Cornelius Melyn

Cornelius Melyn

3rd Patroon of Staten Island, New York

His Children and Some Descendants

Richard Scott Baskas

To order additional copies of this book, contact:
Xlibris Corporation
1-888-795-4274
www.Xlibris.com
Orders@Xlibris.com
47340

CONTENTS

Cornelius' Children and Some Descendants

Born in Amsterdam

Cornelia Melyn

Johannes Melyn

    b. and bapt. by Dr. Baldius 17 April 1629 in Amsterdam, witnessed by Janneken de Vijl; may have been the oldest son (according to the Breeden Raedt) which was lost in the *Princess* shipwreck, on 27 September 1647. While no such statement is made in any of Cornelius Melyn's papers, there is no reason to doubt that he did have a son on the *Princess*, and if so, it would seem probable that it would have been his oldest son who was possibly being taken back to Holland to be educated there. The only other son not accounted for is Abraham who was six years younger than Johannes.

Cornelius Melyn (I)

    b. 3 September 1630; bapt. 6 September 1630 by Dr. Silvius in Amsterdam, witnessed by Maria van Essen; d. before 11 October 1633 Nieuwe Kerk, Amsterdam, Holland as another Cornelius was baptized on that date.

Cornelius Melyn (II)
> b. and bapt. 11 October 1633 in Amsterdam, witnessed by Jacob Reepmaker de Jonge; only mentioned as a casual reference in the Court Records of New Amsterdam, 10 February 1653; killed in September 1655 Staten Island Massacre.

Abraham Melyn
> b. and bapt. 27 May 1635 in Amsterdam by Dr. Clasonius witnessed by Fransoijs de Wael; nothing is known of him unless he was lost in *Princess* shipwreck where he d. September 1647.

Meriken Melyn

Isaack Melyn (I)
> b. and bapt. 21 November 1638 in Amsterdam, witnessed by Jan Melijn; d. before 22 July 1646 Amsterdam, Netherlands as another Isaac was baptized on that date.

Our ancestor   *Born in New Amsterdam*

Susannah Melyn   m. *Johannes/ John/ Jan Winans*
> b. 1643 New Amsterdam, New York; Published by Alice Winans Egy Woolley, *Winans Genealogy, http://cwcfamily.org/egy.htm.*

Magdalen Melyn
> b. before 3 March 1645; bapt. as "Magdaleen Moylin," witnessed by Lijntje Jochems in New Amsterdam; children were Janneken and Jacob.

Forward

Enterestingly enough, this is a remake of the original version. About a year or so after the first one was published, I had realized that it needed to be redone and so in its process, I had found new information. The purpose of compiling information for this book was that in doing research for my own enterest, I had found numerous sources with different information. And so I then decided to take it upon myself to compile this book and hopefully make it history. I also had decided to inclued all his children and about five generations of each.

Cornelius Melyn

I t's enteresting to note that in such a time of chaotic turmoil that one would think that such an individual would have stood out and be noted for their incredible survivalship and continuous journeys in securing a place in time that one would have been recognized in history. His name doesn't really appear to stand out in any type of history, but he became somewhat of an important figure in New Netherland history where he began assisting others in establishing their roots in the New World while also doing the same for himself and his future family. His history is an accompilation of his whole life beginning from his early childhood of setting out on his own as an orphan, his attempts of establishing a home and family in Manhattan and Staten Island, comfronting Peter Stuyvesant, to all the chaotic resiliency he faces to the end.

His real history would begin when he, in the company of others, would encounter his nemesis, Peter Stuyvesant, Dutch Governor of Manhattan, New York, during the attacks of the local Indians in New Sweden and would begin trying to reclaim what was his (Melyn's) plantation along with many other problems that would soon test his inner strength. It was the 17th Century that many Dutch and Belgium settlers immigrated to New Amsterdam, or so sometimes called New Netherland or New Sweden, New York to begin laying claims in the new lands of Staten Island and Manhattan. During this time of establishing a life for themselves and their families, there were many encounters with the local Indians that resulted in having some of their establishments destroyed and some of their families killed. It would be one of the original Staten Island patroons, David Petersen De Vries, who would instigate this destruction by the Indians. One of these settlers who would feel this wrath would be Cornelius Melyn, a Belgium immigrant. After feeling the affects of these Indian attacks perpetrated by De Vries, Melyn would begin organizing a campaign, with the assistance of the Eight Men to lay a case against De Vries. But as De Vries' commission as governor would be replaced by Peter Stuyvesant, Melyn and his associates would begin forming a case against De Vries, demanding for an immediate investigation to these attacks. Stuyvesant soon caught glimpse of these attacks and immediately began formulating a plan to protect himself. Now that he was the new governor of New Netherland, Stuyvesant refused to have these settlers treat him as they did with De Vries. Since Melyn wasn't satisfied with the outcomes of the case against De Vries, Melyn began demanding Stuyvesant to investigate these claims. When it came to handling these Indian attacks, Stuyvesant basically had no interest in this and shrugged it off by stating that he had done all he could in getting rid of the problem. But this of course angered Melyn even more and caused him to slash out more in his campaign against Stuyvesant. Stuyvesant, feeling Melyn's antagonism, felt that the only way to resolve this matter was to rid of Melyn by whatever means.

Antwerp, Belgium

It is believed that the surname Melyn is most likely to have been derived from a former place of residence, probably in the village of Melin, about 60 miles southeast of Antwerp, Belgium, or from De Maline in Flanders. It is known that this family was living in Antwerp in the 16th century. The section of Antwerp that this family was living in was its oldest part. Early Antwerp consisted of a fortified enclosure, the Bourg, which was built on the east bank of the River Scheldt. It appeared as the most prominent feature of the arms of the city. It was built sometime earlier than the middle of the 17th century. The enclosure resembled the letter "D" with the straight side adjacent to the riverbank. A wall of stone enclosing an area about five an a half acres surrounded it and consisted of stone towers at intervals surrounded by a ditch on the land side. At the center of the Bourg stood the Borchtplein, or Plaza, and the Church of Saint Walburga, said to have been the most beautiful church in Antwerp. Extending east from the church to the Bourg wall is a street, "The Sack," so called because it was a blind street, or cul-de-sac. By the 13th century, Antwerp had grown well beyond the immediate vicinity of the Bourg, and a new belt of walls had been constructed further inland so that the wall on the land side of the Bourg was no longer necessary for the purposes of defense. Originally there were two openings in the wall, one about the center of the west or river side, "Werf." This limited means of access had caused great inconvenience, and with the abandonment of the Bourg wall for defensive purposes additional openings were made in the wall, and corresponding bridges thrown across the ditch. One of these openings was at the blind end of "The Sack" which then became Sack Street, being extended a short distance east to connect with existing street on the "mainland." It was in this street, the total length of which was not more than a modern city block, which Cornelis was born. Nearby were the Fosse-du-Borg and the Rue des Sauciers in which the Melyn's lived for a short time afterward. The largest and most striking building with the Bourg wall was the Church of Saint Walburga, commonly called the Borcht Kerck or Castle Church, where Cornelis was baptized. This church, which had its origin in the Chapel of Saint Peter and Saint Peter built sometime before 660 A.D. by Saint Amand, Bishop of Maastricht, was later renamed in honor of Saint Walburga, and was rebuilt in the pointed style in the 13th century. Here it attained the rank of a Parish Church, and from time to time thereafter was enlarged and ornamented until it was said to have been the most beautiful in Antwerp. Above the font there was a painting of the "Last Supper" by Marten de Vos "with two beautiful portraits of _____ Melyn and his wife who gave the piece." There was a portrait of Reverend Franciscus Hovius who was Pastor of the Church in 1618, at the time that Cornelis obtained his certificate of good character. It's unknown of the whereabouts of these two paintings.

Early Life

It was on 17 September 1600 that the would-be-famous Staten Island patroon, Cornelius Melyn, was born in Rue de Sac (Zak Straat or Sack Street), Antwerp, Belgium in a house that was called "The Sack," which was situated in or near the Bourg. He was baptized on his birthday in the Church of St. Walburga with his godparents, Cornelius Lobeyn and Sarah Verreyken. In October of 1606, he lost his mother and on 9 November, he lost his father, therefore, becoming an orphan at the age of six. On 13 November, his uncles, Jacques Melyn and Hans Salomons, took an oath and became his legal guardians through the Orphan Masters of that town. His half-brother, Abraham Melyn, reared him until he was twelve years old. About October 1612, Cornelius' guardians decided that it was time for him to learn a trade in order to earn a living on his own and, therefore, decided to make him a tailor. He was entered in the book of the Guild of Tailors and about January 1613, he was laced as an apprentice with a Thierry (Dirk) Vershulder. As an entrance gift, the guardians presented Vershulder's wife with a fichu, which was paid by seven florins and ten sous. About the end of January or beginning of February of 1613, Jacques died and was replaced as guardian by Abraham, Cornelius' half-brother, for which he took the oath as guardian on 11 February. Cornelius remained about a year in the workshop of Verschulder. About February 1614, the guardians met with the master tailor, Artus van Hembeke, and made a contract with him to teach Cornelius the trade and to furnish him with food and lodging for a sum of 15 florins to be paid yearly by the guardians. This was to be for two years. In February of 1616, Cornelius remained in the workshop. By the time this contract was to expire, it was Artus' turn to compensate Cornelius for his services, which ended up being 20 florins for a year. For the first four years of training, the masters are traditionally paid for providing this training, room and board.

The sedentary life that Cornelius was leading in Antwerp was apparently getting to him, and so he decided to strike out and seek fortune for himself. On 15 September 1618, he announced his intention to see foreign countries by obtaining a copy of his baptismal record from the Priest of the Church he was baptized. He also asked his godfathers, Cornelius Lobyn and Franchoys Ketgen, for a testimonial of good character.

[William J. Hoffman, F.G.B.S. translated this testimony, from a certified copy of the Flemish original]. [1]

At the request of Cornelius Melijn Andriesz, son of the late Andries Melyn and Maria Guedens alias Botens, Cornelius Lobyn, former President of the Carpenters and Lumber Dealers Guild within this City, aged 60 years, and Franchoys Ketgen, Notary, employed as a clerk in the Secretary's office here, aged 50 years, truly swear:

That they well knew the bearer's parents, before named, as legally married people, of good named and reputation, without having heard or learned anything to the contrary in any way, who, among other children, during the aforesaid their wedlock have begotten the a forenamed bearer hereof, born in the house named 'The Sack', situated in the Sack Street here, whom they likewise esteem and hold, and know to be esteemed and held a young man of honor, of good name and reputation, without having heard or learned anything to the contrary in any way; who they well know is not departing from here because of any misconduct; but only [because he] desires to visit [foreign] lands and to learn the languages; alleging as reasons for their knowledge: to wit, the a forenamed Cornelius Lobyns, because he stood sponsor at the font for the a forenamed bere, and the aforesaid Ketgen because he lived I the aforesaid Sack Street opposite the aforesaid 'The Sack', and they, the affiants, have thus associated and conversed often and familiarly with aforesaid bearer, as well as with his parents respectively.

We further certify that the Reverend and master Franciscus Hovius, licentiate in divinity, who has written and signed the certificate to which these our letters are attached, is priest of Saint Walburga's Church here, which is called the Borcht (Castle) Church, and that all ought to give to his writings and instruments perfect credence in legal matters and otherwise.

*In good faith (the literal translation is "without fraud"—a formal
ending to every certificate). The fifteenth of September 1618.*

Cornelius inherited as his share an annual income of 14 florins and
5 sous, being one-third of an income of 42 florins and 15 sous, from a
mortgage placed upon a house named the "Half Moon," situated outside
the Porte-aux-Vauches. According to Antwerp law, he reached majority in
September of 1625 when he became 25. It was customary for one to release
his guardians from their responsibilities with the shortest delay. But Cornelius
was most probably absent from the country at that time, as he did not come
to Antwerp until 2 September 1626 when he compiled with the necessary
formalities of closing his father's estate.

On 22 April 1627, he and Janneken Adryiaens (Van Myert) appeared
before the committee of the Schepens or Aldermen, to apply for their marriage
certificate, which was published. They were married on 9 May 1627 in Nieuwe
Kerk, Amsterdam (one of the major churches of the Dutch Reformed Church
in Holland), North Holland, Holland and after which they both signed it.
Their marriage certificate describes him as a leather dresser living on Elant
Street in Amsterdam. Their marriage license says Jannetjie is "from Myert,
23 years, having no parents, living on the Lingdegracht . . ." The certificate
is now in the Gemeente Archief. When Melyn left Antwerp, he was a tailor's
apprentice, but the certificate has him as a "Seemtouwer" (a dresser of the finer
and softer leathers) showing that he had changed his occupation. Janneken was
born about 1604 in Mydrecht, North Brabant Province in Netherlands and
lived on the Lindenwal. Her last name, Van Myert, is seen as her birthplace
in her certificate. It's not positively identified, but is probably the community
now named Hooge en Lage Mierde (Upper and Lower Mierde) which is
formerly called Myerdt. It is situated in Kempen Land in the Province of
North Brabant, Netherlands, about 14 miles in a generally westerly direction
from Eindhoven, and about 2 miles from the present Belgian frontier.

Illegal Fur Trade

At the baptism of Cornelius' oldest son, Cornelius, in 1633, was Jacob Reepmaker. Reepmaker was one of the directors of the West India Company and a corporate proprietor of New Netherland and of the fur trade of that colony, as well with Germany, Russia and France. They were evidently also interested in the trade because on 23 November 1623, they appointed Hans Joris Hontom as their representative in France, England and Russia. It was at this time that Melyn became involved directly in the fur trade. A document of August 1631 confirms a purchase by Melyn of many moose skins on 29 November 1630, but those skins came from Archangel in Russia. He was also connected with the traders Matheus Heus and Arent Crol, the latter being well known as a fur trader of New Netherland. On 27 September 1633, Jacob Reepmaker appointed Melyn to conduct his affairs at Bayonne in the Pays des Basques, Southern France. On 5 July 1632, Melyn appeared to be in Antwerp as he was the godfather by proxy of Jean Knobbaert, who was at the baptism of Susanne Melyn, daughter of Jean Melyn and Susanne Beert.

In the history of illegal fur trade of Canada, the Basques are very worthy here. They made the life of Champlain and his successors miserable by intruding into the trade wherever they could and by any means possible, selling brandy, muskets and gunpowder. As in early New York history, selling these goods brought Indian problems with war and slaughter to the Europeans. In later 1630, it was no longer easy for the Basques and others to operate in Canada as in Nova Scotia there were still great possibilities for the illegal trade. During the 1630's and 1640's, Nova Scotia was a veritable battleground for any Frenchman who had great ambitions and absolute faith in the future of the fur trade. One opportunist was Cornelius Melyn.

On 30 January 1637, Melyn appeared before Jacob Jacobsen, an Amsterdam Notary. Melyn was mentioned as a merchant of Amsterdam but probably in the city for business. He was accompanied by Basque Adam

Delsaurdi alias Alsatto of St. Jean de Luz, a city near Bayonne. Melyn and Jacobsen had agreed with each other to fish and trade with the natives in Nova Scotia where they bought the ship *Fortuyn* where Delsaurdi would be its captain. The fish and furs would be brought to Amsterdam for sale and after, the proceeds would be divided among them, two-thirds for Melyn and one-third for the Basque. The same proportion was followed in the purchase of the ship. If the journey proved to be successful, they would decide on another enterprise in the same region.

Whether Delsaurdi spent all his money on the buying of the ship is not known. A month later, on 26 February, he appeared before notary Nicolaas Jabcobsen and borrowed from an Amsterdam merchant, Jan Gonsales, four hundred guilders, to be paid twenty days after returning the ship where Melyn was the guarantor of this loan. At the same time, but now in an act drawn up in French, the two entrepreneurs engaged two Basques, Adam de Harenbouren and Jean de Raesen, to assist in the fishing. They were well paid and in advance, which indicates that these men were experienced fisherman and knew the territory.

What happened in the following weeks is unknown. On 17 April 1637, however, Delsaurdi appeared before notary Warnaerts and borrowed from another well-known Amsterdam merchant, Pietr Hustart, the sum of six hundred guilders to be paid back after returning the ship. Again, Melyn and the third portion in the ship and enterprise of Delsaurdi were guarantees for the repayment of the loan and interests.

From the interest of the second loan it appears that the credit of the two partners had gone down steeply during the two months after their initial contract. Furthermore, something remarkable had happened. Delsaurdi had changed his name to something more respectable, in Dutch, and was now called Adam Jansen of St. Jean de Luz. This change probably covered the fact that he didn't speak Dutch.

Again before notary Warnaerts, on 23 April, another act was drawn up. This time Delsaudi (Jansen) would be in charge of the fishing and fur trade only, but Dutchman Willem Claassen of 't Ooch would command the ship and follow a course leading straight to Nova Scotia. Jansen would be considered just another member of the crew and not the owner and outfitter of the third part of the ship and enterprise. It seems these two partners no longer trusted each other. When the ship returned, there was plenty of trouble. Before Warnaerts, on 14 December 1637, Jan Jansen, the captain of the *Fortuyn*, along with Jan Otter, the ship's carpenter and Paulus Mathyssen, the first mate, made a declaration with regard to Delsaurdi's conduct during the journey. They mentioned that four persons of the crew had fished and taken four hundred cod in two hours.

There was plenty of opportunity to catch a good cargo within a short time. This was not so as they had spent too much time on the coast. Delsaurdi had landed many times, staying after for some time to trade with the natives for his profit. He forbade the crew to fish and told them that they were neither capable of fishing nor did they understand how to do it. Apparently Delsaurdi was mostly under the influence and acted like an animal when drunk.

As a partner, the Basque had proved to be a disaster. But Melyn covered himself cleverly. He kept all the merchandise, which had come back with the *Fortuyn* five weeks previously from Canada and paid off the loans contracted by Delsaurdi. It is not mentioned but he probably also kept the third portion, which the Basque had in the ship and was later sold. Melyn financially got the better of the Frenchman. At this point, Delsaurdi seems to have had enough of the Dutch. On 8 January 1644, he left as supercargo of the Cape Breton Company directed by some old French fur traders. It seems that the enterprise had encouraged Melyn to engage himself more in the illegal fur trade and the fishing. On 12 April 1638, he hired the same two Basques sailors who had served on the *Fortuyn*. They worked under his direction on the ship *Wapen van Noorwegen* (*Arms of Norway*) where he went for the fishing of Nova Scotia and the fur trade of New Netherland. This time he didn't trust in foreign partners but went into partnership with Kiliaen van Rensselaer, the ship's owner and financial backer of Melyn.

On 6 May 1638, van Rensselaer notified Wouter van Twiller, Director of New Netherland, and his kinsman that Melyn would be supercargo on the ship, which would sail for New Netherland. On 24 August 1638, van Twiller's successor, Willem Kieft, wrote: [2]

> *While we were sailing in the Bay [of Fundy?] in order to assist the ship Haring we met your ship the Wapen van Noorwegen and we received your letter dated May 7 to which I only can answer with a few lines because of the present circumstances. The bearer of this letter is Cornelius Melyn who is going to Newfoundland or Canada in order to fish and trade there with the natives for furs. May the Lord grant him a prosperous and safe journey.*

On 12 May 1639, van Rensselaer wrote to Kieft: [3]

> *Cornelius Melyn is still in France. He sold there our ship very advantageously but still lacks experience in these matters. He had a*

mediocre catch of fish and did not take more than 12,000 cod. With the years he has to improve himself. At present it costs us money so that he can gain experience.

Melyn had gone back to Rochelle to finish up business and to sell the fish and furs. This was not so unusual since Rochelle was then the center of the Canadian fur trade where ships regularly left for Canada and returned in the fall with the fur harvest of the main trading company, the Company of New France. Rochelle would become one of the main ports of entry for the illegal trade of New Netherland, as is indicated by several Dutch and French notary contracts and the Guyenne Admiralty records of this city. In fact, Melyn had sold his surplus in Manhattan. Only one act of this sale is known to exist, in which one M. Huypodt acknowledged a debt of 135 guilders for two ankers of anisewter. The original receipt became illegible when the *Wapen of Noorwegan* sank in the harbor of Rochelle during her return journey to Patria. The ship was sold at the spot of the disaster to French interested parties who at that time were very shot of shipping. So how much was Melyn worth in 1639? Apparently sufficiently to move to New Netherland where be bought Staten Island and erected a manor there. He seems to have learned fast in the illegal fur trade and knew that the most profitable merchandise in dealing with the natives was brandy. In 1649, Willem Hendricksen testified under oath in Amsterdam that during the winter of 1640 he had been taken into the service of Director Willem Kieft to work for the latter by the month in making brandywine. He lived in Melyn's house where he made his brandy for six to seven weeks and often delivered it to Manhattan. But after that time, Melyn and Kieft had thought it advisable to stop the operation. Hendricksen declared that he had been well paid.

Voyage 1: 1638, Amsterdam, Netherland to New Amsterdam, New York

Before he would begin his journey to the New World, Melyn would leave his wife and family in the Netherlands. She and the rest of their family didn't arrive in New Netherland until 17 May 1641. Cornelis made at least twelve crossings of the Atlantic trying to secure the founding of a colony on Staten Island. The only obligation that was required from foreigners was an oath of allegiance: [4]

> *Cornelius Melyn was possessed of Manorial rights and patronage lordship of the domain of Pavonia Hall, Staten Island in 1640. The family which had also English branches in the name of Mellen, was derived from Malines or De Malines in Flanders. The Lords of Malines descended from Bertold, living in 800, were established as Advocates, or Protectors of Malines, by Bishop of Liege. They were Cavaliers of the Holy Empire in 1721.*

Sometime after 12 May 1638, Cornelius made his first voyage to New Netherland by departing from Texel, (an island in the West Frisians) Amsterdam, Netherlands on the ship *Het Wapen van Noorwegen* (*The Arms of Norway)* that he had purchased. This voyage appeared to have been a reconnaissance mission as he was supercargo. The colony of Rensselaerswyck had a half interest in the ship which on its trip, was so heavily laden that the sailors protested that they would not risk their lives on it. It carried over a number of colonists and a large quantity of goods, including eighteen young mares, thousands of bricks, ironwork, clothing material, spices, cheese, soap, oil and a box filled with earth in which were planted young grape vines. They arrived in the New World on 4 August 1638.

New Netherland, New York

Fort Amsterdam had been built at the south end of Manhattan Island, and a small town, New Amsterdam, had been created for the farmers who brought supplies of military garrison. When Melyn and his colonists arrived on the new land, they would inspect the country. This is when he began conceiving the plan of rounding a colony on Staten Island. Cornelis only spent ten days here before he set sail back to Holland.

Voyage 2: 1638, Newfoundland to France

Melyn departed from Newfoundland on 14 August 1638 on the *Het Wapen van Noorwegen* where some 12,000 codfish were caught. They arrived in France on 12 May 1639 where they sold it with the ship.

Voyage 3: 1639, Amsterdam, Holland to New Netherland

Sometime after 12 May 1639, Melyn departed Holland on the ship *De Liefde* (*The Love*) with its captain, Jan Adriansz Crul.

New Netherland

The ship arrived at New Netherland in late July 1639, only spending six weeks here.

Voyage 4: 1639, New Netherland to Amsterdam, Holland

About 6 September 1639, Melyn departed New Netherlands on one of two ships, *Bryandt van Troyen* or the *Den Harinck* and arrived in Holland before 9 December 1639.

Amsterdam, Holland

To increase immigration to the New World, the Dutch West India Company offered large land grants with feudal authority to wealthy investors (patroons) willing to transport, at their own expense, fifty adult settlers to New Netherlands. Impressed with his own visits to the New World, Cornelius applied for and received a patroonship and Manoral rights for the domain of Pavonia Hall on Staten Island. The Company approved and offered it on 3 July 1640.

Voyage 5: 1640, Holland (ship captured)

About 1 August 1640, Melyn departed Holland on the ship *De Vergulden Hoop* (*The Guilded Hope*) with his people, cattle, goods and all of the implements necessary for agriculture. Unfortunately, on 13 August, the ship was captures by pirates (a Dunkirk frigate) and everything was lost. He promptly decided to make another attempt to colonization where he returned back to Holland. De Vries evidently didn't have a very secure claim to the Island as for 3 July 1640 the West India Company gave Melyn permission to establish a colony there and acknowledged him as a patroon. Dutch farmers permitted livestock to forage freely in the woods where they often invaded unfenced native cornfields. In July 1640, Director General Willem Kieft sent 100-armed men to punish the Raritan Indians when some pigs disappeared on Staten Island. The expedition ended up killing several Raritan, including a sachem (chief). On 1 September, the Indians retaliated, killing four Dutch settlers and burned all the buildings, wiping out Staten Island's first settlement. On 18 February 1641, Melyn applied to the Company for a renewal, or confirmation, of his Patroonship, which was granted on 25 February. While he was in Holland, trouble was brewing in New Netherland because the Dutch colonists did not treat the native tribes well. Before Cornelis ever took physical possession of his patroonship, Melyn sold a half interest in his Island project to Godert (or Godard) van Reede, Lord of Nederhorst, a Deputy in the States General, on 16 May in order to finance his expedition. This created for him not only in obtaining financial assistance, but also a powerful protector. This agreement was evidently the formal conclusion of previous negotiations, as Melyn sailed back to New Netherland with a new part of colonists. He and his party of forty-one colonists were soon hard at work on the Island, where they "immediately began to build house, to plough land, and to do everything conducive to establishing a good colony, begrudging neither money nor labor." [5]

> In manner and on conditions hereafter expressed the Very Noble Jongheer (Lord) Godert Van Reede, Lord of Nederhorst, etc., has agreed with Cornelis Melyn that the said Lord of Nederhorst shall receive and possess in ownership the just half of the colonies acquired by Cornelis Melyn from the West India Company on Staten Island or elsewhere to be selected as well in regard to jurisdiction as to ownership of the lands, woods, and all other rights, appertaining to the said colony. Which one half said Melyn by these presents cedes to the Lord of Nederhorst; the other half as well as in regard to jurisdiction, lands, woods and rights appertaining to the same remaining to the said Cornelis Melyn; provided that said colony with the consent and approbation of both parties, shall be divided in two equal parts, an exact map of which shall be made and sent over by the said Melyn, to be then drawn for by the said Lord of Nederhorst, and by the said Melyn. And in case the said Lord of Nederhorst should draw the part upon which said Melyn

*should have incurred any expenses, said Lord of Nederhorst in such case
shall pay indemnification, upon the award of expert arbitrators. With
the distinct understanding that each for his own share shall bear his
won expenses and shall people the same, and further each shall regulate
his won property in such a manner as they shall deem proper without
having anything further in community with the other; with express
condition that if the Lord Count of Solms in regard to his Colony should
happen to acquire any more privileges from the West India Company or
their High Mightinesses, that said Lord of Nederhorst shall also exert
himself as much as possible that said Melyn, in such case, shall also
receive similar condition and privileges for his portion, without however
being obliged to positively acquire the same. Said Melyn promising to
act as superintendent and to take care that the people to be sent there by
the Lord of Nederhorst (who will do so as soon as his Honor shall find
an opportunity) shall be held to their duty, and to report on the same
from time to time. The said people to be sent there by the said Lord
of Nederhorst are not to act in weighty matters unless with the advice
of the said Cornelis Melyn. In ratification of which parties mutually
pledge their respective persons and goods, submitting the same for this
purpose to all Lords, Courts and jurisdictions. In testimony respective
parties have subscribed to this present (which remains in the custody
of me Jan De Graeff Notary Public at Amsterdam) in the presence of
and with me Notary, at Amsterdam, this sixth of May, old style, of the
year sixteen hundred forty one.*

*Agrees with the minute of the deceased Notary Jan De Graeff, this
16th January Anno 1648.*

*By me
F. Steur, Notary Public 1648.*

Voyage 6: 1641, Amsterdam, Holland, family immigrates with him to New Netherland

Melyn set sail from Holland on the ship, *Den Eyckenboom* (*The Oak Tree*), in 17 May 1641 with his wife and children and arrived in New Netherland on 14 August. Melyn's family was located somewhere along the Barrows, most probably near Fort Wadsworth. De Vries claims that on 20 August of Melyn's arrival, the Island belonged to him. On 19 June 1642, Kieft gave Melyn his formal patent for "the entire Staten Island" except for only a farm, which Kieft had granted to De Vries before the Company had allotted the Island to Melyn. Melyn would become its third patroon.

The Twelve Men

Due to constant Indian problems, which would lead to the Indian War of 1641, New Netherland would most likely not exist. To prevent this from happening, Governor Kieft called together a board of what would become the "Twelve Men," including Melyn, to consider new ways of dealing with the Indians and bring about new policies and proposals. On 21 January 1642, the Twelve Men sent a petition to Kieft designating themselves as "selectmen on behalf of the Commonality of New Netherland," hoping to establish a voice in the affairs of the colony.

Whiskey War of 1642, Melyn flees to New Amsterdam

Despite Melyn's political character against Kieft's policies, Kieft asked Melyn to build him America's first whiskey distillery in what is known today as New Brighton. The settlers taught the local Indians to drink whiskey. In other words, when the Indians got drunk, the settlers took advantage of them. The Indians became angry, eventually killing many of the Dutch farmers and burning their homes. Melyn's settlement was destroyed by Indians during this "Whiskey War" in 1642. Melyn later fled to New Amsterdam. On 29 June, Director General Kieft granted him a "ground brief" or patent, covering all of Staten Island except De Vries' reserved "bouwerij" and investing him with all the powers, jurisdictions, privileges and pre-eminence as a patroon. [6]

> We Willem Kieft, Director General and Councillors in behalf of the High Mighty Lords States General of the United Netherlands, his Highness of Orange and the Hon. Managers of the General Privilege West India Company, residing in New Netherland: Make known that on his underwritten date we have given and granted as we are giving and granting by these presents (by virtue of a certain Act, dated July 1640, conceded by said Lords Managers) to Cornelius Melyn the entire Staten Island, situated on the bay and North River of New Netherland, excepting so much land as appertains to a farm which by us Director and Councillors before mentioned had been granted and given-before the date of the before mentioned Act to David Peterse De Vries of Hoorn, which land has also been occupied by him, David

Peterse; all under express conditions that he, Coenelius Melyn, or those by virtue of the present entering upon his rights, shall acknowledge the said Hon. Heeren managers as their Lords, under the Sovereignty of the High Mighty Lords the States General; and hereto obey their Director and Councillords as good inhabitants are bound to do; providing he, Melyn, or those entering upon his right submit in whole and in part to all such charges and requisitions as—in accordance with the exemptions of New Netherland-have been already levied or shall yet be levied by the Managers; consequently constituting in quality and by virtue as expressed before, said Cornelius Melyn, in our stead, real and actual possessor of the aforesaid parcel of land; granting him by these presents, perfect power, authority and special order to take possession of, cultivate, inhabit, use the said Staten Island-except the said farm-as he may do with other his patrimonial lands and effects, without we, the grantors, in the aforesaid quality are reserving or retaining any the least share, claim or authority in the same, desisting of the same in behalf of as above.

The location of this plantation is said to have been at "Tompkinsville" at or near the "watering place" where vessels on their way to sea stopped for water and wood. This place is shown in the 1797 Staten Island map (a copy is in the Staten Island Institute of Arts and Sciences' collection). It is described as "the small rivulet called the watering place," and shown in detail on the Map of Quarantine Property, 1799 (filed in the office of the County Clerk as Map No. 1). This rivulet (no longer exists), fed, it is said, by a spring, was less than two hundred feet north of Arietta Street, Tompkinsville, and its outlet was a short distance east of the present railway. It is quite probably that the entire neighborhood of this outlet became known as the "Watering Place."

It appears that Melyn may have had a female servant as on 11 September 1642, he was brought into court to reclaim his "property." He brought suit against an Egbert Wouterszen, husband and guardian of Engel Jans, her mother, for damages on account of Elsje's marriage engagement before her term of service to him had expired. On the trial, she testified that her mother and another woman had brought the young man to Staten Island whom she had never seen before, and desired her to marry him. She declined at first, as she did not know him, and had no inclination to marry, but finally consented. She concluded by returning the pocket-handkerchief she received as a marriage present. On 16 October, she declared that she sent for Adrian Pietersen and that on his coming to the Island she accompanied him on board his yawl. A week later, Melyn and the Fiscal had Pietersen before the court charged with Elsje's abduction. Pietersen was ordered to bring her into court, deliver her to Melyn, and receive her again from him on giving security for the payment of any damages that Melyn may have suffered. [7]

Indian War of 1643

Trouble with the Indians began about 1640 when De Vries' bouwery was attacked and the measures that Kieft took only further enraged the Indians against Kieft and the Dutch. These troubles led to the Indian War of 1643. From 1643 to 1645, "Governor Kieft's War" against about twenty tribes of local Indians rampaged around Manhattan and Staten Island. More than 2,500 lives were lost. Kieft had decided to exterminate one tribe by setting an example to the other Wilden (wild men) near Manhattan. On the night of 25 February 1643, his men made two surprise attacks on the sleeping villages near Pavonia and, without regard for sex or aged, massacred at least 110. As word of the "Pavonia Massacre" reached the other tribes along the lower river, they retaliated with attacks. One of them, of the Weckquaskeek tribe, murdered a white man. The government demanded that the tribe surrender their murderer. Governor Kieft was looking for an opportunity to exterminate the Indians. A savage massacre resulted as the majority of the white population would not have a war with the Indians. Melyn's colony was saved for a time, but late 1643, it was attacked, leaving everything in ruins. This frustrated Melyn's design to establish a settlement and held Kieft responsible. Melyn took his family to Manhattan Island, where he bought a home to be used as temporary lodging during the troubled times.

The Melyn House, Manhattan

On 24 October 1643, when Long Island and even Manhattan Island "north of the Fresh Water" (about the present Duane Street) were practically laid waste, "Staten Island, where Cornelius Melyn settled, is unattacked as yet, but stands hourly expecting an assault." Due to the Indian attacks, the Melyn family was forced to cross the North River and seek refuge near the fort on lower Manhattan near where the "canal" (ditch) drained into the East River, and built a two-story house on it. [8]

In the year after the birth of our Lord and Savior Jesus Christ one thousand six hundred four and forty the 17th day of December, appeared before me Cornelis Van Tienhoven, Secretary of New Netherland, Burger Jorisen, Farrier (hoefsmid) and inhabitant here, who declared in the presence of the below subscribed witnesses to convey and transfer in a true free ownership to Mr. Cornelis Melyn, his house and lot situated on the island Manhatans, as he is by these presents conveying and transferring said lot and house by virtue of ground brief & conveyance granted by the Director and Councillors of New Netherland, dated April 28, 1643. On account whereof he Burger Jorisen Constitutes in his stead as real and actual owner of the said lot and house said Cornelis Melyn or those entering upon his right, granting him irrevocable power, authority and what has been expressed before, so that he, Melyn, may do with and dispose of the same as he might do with other his patrimonial estate, without he, and grantor, retaining in the same any ownership or claim (the bill of sale having been satisfied), but renouncing the same from now on for ever. In testimony hereof, the Minute of the present has been subscribed to at the record office by Burger Jorissen, Will. De Kay & Gysbert Opdyck, as witnesses invited for this purpose. Done at Fort Amsterdam in New Netherland, December 17, 1644, New Style. It was subscribed to with the mark of Burger Jorisen and signed in the name of Burger Jorisen.

On March 18, 1661 the here standing name has been put down by Burger Jorisse. To which we testify N. De Sille, N. Bayard

A true copy taken from the Records being much toorne. (signed) David Jamison. D:Secry. Endorsed in Dutch: Conveyance of Burger Joris to Cornelis Meyln, December 17th, 1644.

Melyn received a grant of a double lot in Manhattan on 28 April 1643 . . . [9]

We, William Kieft Director General and Councillors for the High Mighty Lords States General of the United Netherlands, his Highness of Orange and the Hon. Heeren managers of the privileged West India Company, residing in New Netherland, Make known and declare by these presents that on this underwritten date we have granted to Burger Joorissen a lot situated on the bank of the East River on the Island Manhatans to the East of the Fort, extending to the East eleven rods and to the North ten rods, being an uneven square amounting to one hundred and ten rods of land; with express conditions and stipulations that he, Borger Joorisen, or those acquiring by virture of this present his right, shall acknowledge the aforesaid

Heeren Managers as his Lords and Patroons under the Sovereignty of the High Mighty Lords States General, and here their Director and Councillors to obey in everything as good inhabitants are bound to do; and provided he, Burger Joorisen further submits to all such charges and duties as have already been imposed or shall yet be imposed by the Hon. Heeren. It is also stipulated that Burger Joorissen, in one or two years time, on the said lot on the strand shall yet cause to be built a good house. Therefore conferring upon said Burger Jorissen, or those entering upon his right in our stead real and actual ownership of said lot, granting him by these presents absolute and irrevocable power and authority and special order to build on, inhabit, and use said lot, as he might do with other his patrimonial lands and possessions, without we grantors, in our afore stated quality, having, reserving or retaining any the least share, ownership or authority in the same, but in behalf of as above from now on and forever renouncing everything, promising further firmly irrevocably and unbreakably to observe and carry out this their Conveyance, all under pledge as expressed by law; without guile or craft this had been subscribed by us and condirmed with our seal in red wax, in Fort Amsterdam April 28th, New Style.

Was signed William Kieft.
By order of the Hon. Heeren Directors and Councillors of New Netherland
Cornelis van Tienhoven
Secretary
Lib A fo. 58
A true Copy
David Jamison D: Secry
Endorsed in Dutch
Grant of Burger Jorison, of the 28th April 1643.

It was soon after that he would meet his new neighbor, Jochem Kuyter, a German who had served in the Danish navy in the East Indies and then searched for a more peaceful refuge, settled in Manhattan in 1639. Both had experienced Indian attacks and property damage. They soon started sharing notes of their loses and eventually decided to launch an offensive attack against Kieft and the Company. On 3 November 1643, the citizens wrote to the States General: [10]

*Almost every place is abandoned. We, wretched people, must skulk with
wives and little ones that still survive, in poverty together, in and around
the fort at the manhattans where we are not safe, even for an hour.*

Melyn's patent covered the east half of the present Broad Street from the south
line of Hoogh Street, extending west, south of "the shore of the East River."
Here he built a two-story brick house. In 1643, he received a ground-brief
of . . . [11]

*. . . about 62 English feet in front along the road, which with bridge
lay north of it and it extended in depth about 88 English feet to the
river shore; through it the stream or ditch from Blommarerts Vly ran
into the East River.*

Cornelius then states . . .

*I was obliged to flee for the sake of saving my life, and to sojourn with
wife and children at the Menatans till the year 1647.*

These three adjoining pieces of property were then located near the
intersection of Broad and Pearl Streets, the latter being on the shore of the East
River at the time. This property was bounded north and south respectfully by
the present Stone and Pearl Streets and extended easterly from Broad Street in
the direction of Coenties Alley. In August 1644, he bought one house for 250
guilders and in December, bought another for 950 guilders. That year, Kieft
offered 25,000 guilders to the English in Connecticut for 150 men to help
put down the Indian uprising. The combined forces crushed the natives. In
1645, he was charged with selling wine to the Indians, but nothing appeared
to have come about this.

The Eight Men

The Indian attacks had caused such anarchy that Kieft had proposed
having a new council of representatives to assist him in restoring order in his
government and would pick those who he felt would support him. Melyn was
picked, since it was thought that Melyn might be grateful to the company
for being given such an opportunity for advancement. Once Melyn settled
into Manhattan, he became the leader of this group. The Council of Eight,
or the Eight Men, met with Kieft several times, but Kieft wouldn't listen to

their recommendations. On 24 October 1643, the Eight Men sent a letter (supposedly by Melyn) to . . . [12]

> *The Honorable, Wise, Prudent Gentlemen of the XIX of the General Incorporated West India Company at the Chambers at Amsterdam praying for immediate and decisive help.*

On 3 November, they sent a Memorial to . . . [13]

> *The Honorable, High and Mighty Lords, The Noble Lords, The States General of the United Netherlands Provinces. We have had no means of defense provided against a savage foe, and we have had a miserable despot sent out to rule over us.*

On 18 June 1644, Kieft assembled the group, including his secretary, Cornelis van Tienhoven. Tienhoven wasn't yet a member of the board but was probably present at the meeting. He first stated that the colony had no money due to the war. He proposed raising the money by taxing beavers and beer. The crowd obviously roared with anger. How can such a population be treated this way especially loosing their property due to the war. Even if they were able to pay these taxes, they would refuse. They argued that taxation without authorization from the company in Amsterdam was unlawful. Kieft roared with anger, "I have more power here than the company!" This made Kuyter even more angry and then threatened Kieft that he would "certainly have him." The meeting broke up into chaos and sometime later, Kieft's soldiers were placing announcements all over town stating the new taxes. On 28 October 1644, the Eight Men addressed in a Memorial sent by the "Blue Cock" to the West India Company, charge the whole blame of the war upon Kieft and demanded his recall. They also warned the Company against Kieft regarding his book that contained the origin of the war "as many lies as lines" and "as few facts as leaves."

Desiring to control more land in this vicinity then his original small plot, Melyn bought the house of Eben Reddenhause for 250 guilders, or about $100 in August 1644. He also bought the house of Burger Jorissen in December 1644 for 950 guilders, or $380, so that now he owned all the land along the river from "the ditch" to the City Tavern.

Melyn and Kuyter, having sustained numerous loses, knew that the government, with Kieft at the hand, was to blame. Its policy dealing with the Indians had brought disaster to the whites. So they made their influence

felt against Kieft and worked for a better government. In order to increase
the finances of the West Indian Company, Director Kieft imposed an excise
upon the wines and spirits at the rate of four stivers per quart, likewise upon
every beaver skin one guilder. In proclaiming this, Kieft opposed to the Eight
Men. They claimed that imposing taxes was an act of sovereignty which the
Company did not possess and that the hiring and keeping of soldiers was the
company's business and not of the settlers. Kieft was rude in dealing with the
Eight Men. He once snubbed the board by summoning three of its members,
Kuyter, Melyn and Hal, to appear a certain day at eight o'clock in the morning.
They came and waited till past noon. Kieft had gone off somewhere on other
business, and the three finally went off "as wise as they came." Another error
of Kieft's was that once when the brewers refused to pay the taxes, he caused
sundry casks of liquor to be confiscated and handed over to thirsty soldiers!
After six months of wrangling, the Eight Men sent their eloquent "Memorial"
to the States General. They described the condition of the country and
registered their gravamina. The petition asked for a new governor and for
some limitation of his power by representatives of the people. [14]

28 October 1644 Memorial

Our fields lie fallow and waste; our dwellings and other buildings
are burned; not a handful can be either planted or sown this autumn
on the deserted places; the crops which God permitted to come forth
during the past summer remain on the fields standing and rotting; . . .
we have no means to provide necessaries for wives or children; and we
sit here amid thousands of barbarians, from whom we find neither
peace nor mercy . . . . There are among us those who . . . for many
long years have endeavoured at great expense to improve their lands
and villages; others, with their private capital, have equipped with all
necessaries their own ships; some, agains, have come hither with ships
independent of the Company, freighted with a large quantity of cattle,
and with a number of families; who have erected handsome buildings
on the spots selected for their people, cleared away the forest, enclosed
their plantations and brought them under the plough, so as to be an
ornament to the country and a profit to the proprietors, after their long
laborious toil. The whole of these now lie in ashes through a foolish
hankering after war. For all right-thinking men here know that these
Indians have lived as lambs among us, until a few years ago . . . . These
hath the Director, by various uncalled-for proceedings, so embittered

*against the Netherlands nation, that we do not believe that anything
will bring them and peace back, unless the Lord, who bends all men's
hearts to his will, should propitiate them.*

The Memorial continues on explaining the origin and progress of the war,
the Director's method of government and also warns the States General
against putting their trust in an elaborate report that Kieft sent over to The
Hague. [15]

*If we are correctly informed by those who have seen it, it contains as
many lies as lines.*

The Eight Men concluded their petitions: [16]

*Honored Lords, this is what we have, in the sorrow of our hearts, to
complain of; that one man who has been sent out, sworn and instructed
by his lords and masters, to whom he is responsible, should dispose here
of our lives and property according to his will and pleasure, in a manner
so arbitrary that a king would not be suffered legally to do. We shall
end here, and commit the matter wholly to our God, who, we pray and
heartily trust, will move your Lordships' minds and bless your Lordships'
deliberations, so that one of these two things may happen-either that a
Governor may be speedily sent with a beloved peace to us, or that their
Honours [i.e. the Company] will be pleased to permit us to return,
with wives and children, to our dear Fatherland. For it is impossible
ever to settle this country until a different system be introduced here,
and a new Governor be sent out with more people, who shall settle
themselves in suitable places, one near the other, in form of villages
and hamlets, and elect from among themselves a bailiff, or schout, and
schepens, who shall be empowered to send deputies to vote on public
affairs with the Director and Council; so that hereafter the Country
may not be again brought into similar danger.*

In the meantime, Kuyter had been forced to move to New Amsterdam on
account of the burning his bowery house and later purchased a small house
at the corner of Pearl and Broad Street. His former neighbor, Melyn, proved
a faithful ally to him. Melyn and the Eight Men addressed Memorials to the
States-General of the Netherlands and to the Company regarding their affairs
and the ravages of the Indians . . . [17]

. . . daily in our houses and fields have they cruelly murdered men and women, and with hatchets and tomahawks struck little children dead in their parents' arms or before their doors, or carried them away into bondage; the houses and grain barracks are burnt with the produce; cattle of all descriptions are slain and destroyed, and such as remain must perish this approaching winter for want of fodder. Almost every place is abandoned . . . We wretched people must skulk with wives and little ones that still survive in poverty together, in and around the fort at Manhattans, where we are not safe even for an hour.

It appears that this was to be taken as a threat as it wasn't advised further; "Should suitable assistance not arrive (contrary to our expectations), we shall through necessity, in order to save the lives of those who remain, be obliged to betake ourselves to the English at the East, who would like nothing better than to possess this place."

That same year, Melyn had leased about two acres of ground from the officers of the Company, covering the site of the present Trinity Church and the northern portion of the churchyard, and extending to the river bank, for raising grain, eventually for his family's use. On 31 May 1646, Kieft and his Council pettishly alleged that Melyn . . . [18]

. . . having planted and fenced a pieced a land north of the Company's garden, taking in more ground than belonged to him, sweeping away with a curve behind said garden, and making use of the sods and earth of the Company's soil for security of said land,' ordered that 'he may cut his grain, and then deliver up the Company's ground in the same condition as in the Spring.

Melyn soon sold his house, on Pearl and Broad Streets, to Seger Teunissen, who was later killed by Indians. Seger had some property that was left behind and was confiscated and sold according to Kieft's order. After four years of letter writing, investigations and committee pondering, action was taken . . . [19]

Cornelis Melyn was the first great democrat of this country. This is not, of course, in the sense of a democrat opposed to a republican candidate at the polls but one who favors a government controlled by the people, or one who believes in political and legal equality.

Due to Kieft having to introduce tools, excises and imposts in order to obtain whatever means he could to support the war, the Eight Men, Joachim Pietersz-Keuyter, Cornelis Melyn, Isaac Allerton, Jacob Stoffelsz, Gerrit Wolfertz, Thomas Hall, Jan Evertsz-Bout and Barent Dircksz, sent a letter to the Chamber of Amsterdam filing their complaint. The College of XIX sent Kieft back a copy of what the members had written and what was written to him and did what he could to protect himself.

Stuyvesant replaces Kieft

On 28 July 1646, The College of XIX, the nineteen managers of the West India Company, its governing body, finally decided to recall Kieft. Stuyvesant received his commission as Director-General and reached New Amsterdam on 11 May 1647. When Kieft surrendered his government, he asked the people to give his administration their formal endorsement. All the citizens, especially Kuyter and Melyn, refused. As Kieft was delivering his departing speech, Kieft mistakenly paused while giving the community a chance to thank him in return. The pause allowed Kuyter to exchange a few of his thoughts and at the same time, Melyn added a few of his own. Melyn and Kuyter both came forward with a petition for a judicial inquiry into Kieft's policy and behavior since 1639 when he first tried to impose taxes upon the Indians. They wished to propound a series of interrogatories and intended to base upon these answers a report that would be carried to Holland and used as a weapon against him. Kieft came forward and accused them of being the real authors of the memorial which the Eight Men had sent the Company, which led to his removal. Since Stuyvesant was in the crowd, the noise suddenly stopped and everyone looked at him. Stuyvesant had already been apprised of the situation regarding Kieft and was more aware of it than Kieft himself. Due to Stuyvesant's military experience, he was well brought up in knowing of his precedent and those that were against Kieft, namely Melyn and Kuyter.

Stuyvesant seemed to have realized what could possibly happen if such matters were carried out against Kieft and saw that it could also happen to him in the future. He immediately took Kieft's part and declared that the officers of the government must not be obliged to disclose government secrets simply on the demand of two private citizens. To petition against one's rulers was treason. Stuyvesant replaced Kieft on 27 May 1647 at Fort Amsterdam. The whole community was present and listened with eagerness to Stuyvesant's well-prepared speech. According to Melyn . . . [20]

He kept the people standing with their heads uncovered for more than an hour, while he wore his 'chapeau,' as if he were the Czar of Muscovy.

During those few days of being sworn into his new office, Stuyvesant marched around town with a copy of the October 1644 letter that was sent by the colonists, in the names of Jochem Kuyter and Cornelius Melyn, demanding Kieft's recall. Strangely enough, it had served its purpose. But in the meantime, it had also brought about a man who looked on such acts as treason.

Melyn and Kuyter charged with treason

Within a few days of Kieft leaving office, Melyn and Kuyter, representing the Eight Men, brought a formal complaint against Kieft and asked for an inquiry in the abuses of his late government and respecting his treatment of the Indians. Because of his autocratic nature and military training, Stuyvesant refused any requests for any investigations. He considered them merely as "perturbators of the public peace" and the Director-General and Council declined to go even further with the complaint. After seeing that Stuyvesant was on his side, Kieft brought criminal charges against Melyn and Kuyter on 18 June 1647. Stuyvesant served the bench while Judge Van Dincklagen sat next to him. Lawyers were rare in this city and so the prisoners had to defend for themselves. They were arrested on a charge of "rebellion of sedition" and they coerced others into joining in these charges. Stuyvesant had intended this trial to be swift and decisive, where the two parties would sit quietly and listen to him lay out the situation and render his judgment. He was stunned to receive a list of questions and demands that was to be posed to the parties and a call for the reorganization of the colony. He ordered a hasty end to the session, after having read through the documents that evening and the next day, he then reconvened. Stuyvesant's counsel agreed that "evil consequences" would definitely come about if the two colonists were allowed to proceed in framing a legal argument against the administration. Stuyvesant rejected out of hand the notion that Kuyter and Melyn acted as representatives through original board of the Eight Men that Kieft had called together. Kuyter and Melyn both complained that Stuyvesant and his council were prejudiced in favor of Kieft and the Company and that what verdict was rendered would be tainted. Stuyvesant then produced the letter to Kieft, even Kieft had never seen. Kieft grew with rage as he read it. Stuyvesant had counted on this reaction. Kieft then wrote a formal complaint, declaring that Kuyter and Melyn had endeavored "with false and bitter poison, to calummate their magistrates and to bring them into difficulty." Complaining that they had "dispatched in an irregular manner and clandestinely sent off, that libelous letter" and demanded that they be prosecuted and that his name be cleared. This is what Stuyvesant needed in order to move forward. He sent a messenger running down Pearl Street to Melyn and Kuyter's houses with a copy of Kieft's letter and an order that they submit a response within forty-eight hours. They were summoned to show cause why they should not be banished "as pestilent and seditious persons" but they were determined to go "as good patriots and proprietors in New Netherland." Melyn and Kuyter were given twenty-four hours to reply. They got together to prepare their answer, which had to be done in secrecy. Tienhoven's house stood right next to Kuyter's and Melyn's house along the East River shore. If there was a time to back down, to respond gingerly and throw themselves on the mercy of the new director-general, it was now. They choose the opposite tack. And so their letter of 22 June 1647 was "long, legalistic, courtly, precise and unflinching . . . pure Van der Donck." Because their defense was so well prepared and written, and with so many quotations from many classical authors, that it appeared that Adriaen van der Donck, a former student at Leiden University and a friend and ally of Melyn and Kuyter, had represented them in court. The letter is composed of four parts of legal protocol and is addressed to Stuyvesant and his council . . . [21]

Honorable Gentlemen!

The written demand of the late Director General Kieft was sent to us by the Court messenger about 9 o'clock on the 19th June of this year, 1647, with express orders to answer thereunto within twice 24 hours. Coming then to the point— . . .

. . . The piles of ashes from the burnt houses, barns, barracks and other buildings, and the bones of the cattle, more than sufficiently demonstrate the ordinary care that was bestowed on the country, God help it, during the war . . .

. . . The agreeing to the excise is seen by 3 letters, E., F., G.; by the Acts of the 18, 21, 22 June, 1644, and therefore no further declaration is necessary . . .

. . . It is chiefly manifest from their own act, that the Indians conducted themselves like lambs, before the melancholy spectacle of which they

were the victims in the year 1643 over at Pavonia and on the Island
Manhatas. Be it remarked, that they allowed themselves, their wives
and children to be slaughtered at that time like sheep, and came (so to
speak) like lambs to lie in our arms. We appeal in this case to the entire
Commonality and to each member of it individually, who hath survived
that time, to say how murderously the Indians were then treated. Would
to God we may be found to be liars on this point . . .

Because of his well-prepared defense, Kieft had to take up a new line of
proceeding. They boldly reiterated the charges and offered to bring forward
the four survivors of the Eight Men to testify that these had signed the charges
against Kieft of their own will and not through the influence of the persons
accused. [22]

Indictments were brought against Kuyter and Melyn on sundry
trumped-up charges alleging treacherous dealings with the Indians and
attempts to stir up rebellion. With shameless disregard of evidence, a
prearranged verdict of guilty were rendered.

They did admit that in the heat of war and due to the loss of their property,
they had complained to Holland. Unfortunately they had been prejudged and
found guilty and capital punishment was for a time, seriously contemplated.
Stuyvesant had suggested that Melyn be put to death and that Kuyter be
banished and his property be confiscated. When Melyn asked for a stay of
sentence, until he could appeal to the States, General Stuyvesant is said to
have thundered . . . [23]

People may think of appealing during my time-should any one do so,
I would have him made a foot shorter, pack the pieces off to Holland
and let him appeal in that way.

Due the urges of his council, Stuyvesant amended his sentences for both and
gave them the opportunity to appeal and ordered them to depart by the first
available ship. Fearing the worst, Melyn deeded his house to his daughter,
Cornelia Melyn-Loper on 11 July 1647. [24]

Whereas Cornelis Melyn, born at Antwerp, about forty-five years of
age, an inhabitant of New Amsterdam, in new Netherland, dared,
as is proven by statements under oath, to oppose and violate justice,

on the 2d of May, 1645, and to threaten the Director-General, Kieft, then his governor and chief magistrate, with the gallows and wheel, or, as the delinquent, prevaricating but voluntarily confessing, admitted that he said to the attorney-general and others, "They who have given such orders [in relation to the Indian war] may be upon their guard that they come neither to the gallows nor on the wheel," and to oppose himself further to the orders of Director Kieft, so that the Attorney-general was obliged to protest of contumacy and opposition against said Melyn: And as said Melyn is, by sundry other statements under oath at different times, convicted of abusing the court, saying, that there was no justice here: that he was not subject to the director-general; that the director-general might look after the company's servants; that he was the devil's head, with numerous mutinous and seditious words to divers soldiers and freemen, endeavoring to persuade the servants of the company to leave its service, because they would not receive their pay; that the governor was the greatest liar in the country, who gave many fair words and promises, but never performed them; and also of instigating the freemen not to pay what they owed; and of many other acts of the same kind, as if proven by various affidavits and credible witnesses, all of which were distinctly read to said Melyn; and also of robbing or endeavoring to steal from the Indians on Long Island at the beginning of the war, in which they did not participate, their corn, in a clandestine or forcible manner, on which occasion an Englishman was shot by the said Indians; which fact, notwithstanding his denial, appears from his own confession in open court on the 16th of January of this year, when he admitted that his servants, with some soldiers, planned the expedition, but against his orders; of which, however, he never made any complaint, nor informed any court of what had happened, which is sufficient proof that he connived at the transaction, and by his silence approved of it; and also of compelling the Indians of Staten Island to surrender to him a part of their hunting-grounds, as appears by statements under oath on the last day of July, 1645;-all which doings are of a pernicious tendency, leading to mutiny and rebellion, defamation of justice, and of the chief magistrate, and encouraging violence: To all this must be added that he, Melyn, with one Jochem Petersen Kuyter, conceived and wrote a letter on the 28th of October, 1644, in the name of the eight elect men, which they copied, signed, and sent to the Honorable Directors of the West India Company of the Chamber of Amsterdam, as calumnious as false, wherein they, in the most face and scandalous manner, abuse and insult the Hon. Director Kieft, then their governor and chief magistrate, as may be seen and read in the original,-the which being examined and investigated at the request of the aforesaid Director Kieft, We declare that said letter is false in its principal points, as is confirmed by his voluntary confession, by the evidence of as many as fifteen others, and by the declarations and answers of several who signed the letter: Whereupon the attorney-general instituted proceedings against the said Melyn, and convicted him of having committed the crime of defamation against the court and justice, and falsehood in writing, and consequently of being guilty of the crime of loesoe majestais. All which facts, proofs, and documents having been examined, and every part duly considered by the Hon. Director and Council, It is their opinion that such misdeeds are of the most serious and alarming consequences under any well-regulated government, where they ought not be cannot be tolerated, but ought to be exemplarily punished; Wherefore the director-general, Petrus Stuyvesant, with the advice of the members of his council, administering justice in the name and in behalf of their High and Mighty Lords, the States General, his Highness the Prince of Orange, and the Noble Directors of the privileged West India Company, does condemn the aforesaid Cornelis Melyn to be banished for seven years from the limits of the jurisdiction of New Netherland, to depart with the first sailing vessel, revoking and withdrawing all benefices, pretensions, and honors which he owed to said directors, and in addition sentencing him to pay an amend of three hundred Carolus guilders, to be distributed, one-third to the poor, one-third to the church, and one-third to the attorney-general, and rejecting the other parts of the said attorney's conclusions. Done in Council in Fort Amsterdam, 23d July, 1647. (Sd.) P. Stuyvesant, L. van Dincklage, Brian Newton, Pouwelis Leenders van der Grift, Jan Claessen Boll.

Stuyvesant and his Council decided to have them both sentenced on 25 July 1647. Melyn was accused of embracing treason, bearing false witness, libel and defamation. He was sentenced to seven years' banishment and fined 300 guilders. Kuyter was accused of "raising his finger in a threatening manner" to Kieft and sentenced to three years' banishment and fined 150 guilders. The fines were to be given one-third to the attorney general, one-third to the church, and one-third to the poor. The prisoners were required to sign a written promise that, in any place to which they might go they would never complain, or speak in any way, of what they had suffered from Kieft and Stuyvesant. An eyewitness account say that they were "brought on board like criminals and torn away from their goods, their wives and their children." Stuyvesant did try before to have Melyn beheaded but the governor's council did see it inappropriate. His feelings towards Melyn seemed as " . . . if I were persuaded you would appeal from my sentences, or divulge them, I would have your head cut off, or have you hanged on the highest tree in New Netherland."

Voyage 7: 1647, New Netherlands to Holland (Ship Wreck)

A few months after Stuyvesant arrived at the fort, Kieft set sail for Holland, along with Melyn and Kuyter, as his prisoners on 16 August 1647 on the ship *Princess Amelia*. The Rev. Dominic Bogardus, minister at Manhattan from 1633 to 1647, victims of Kieft's and Stuyvesant's persecution—Kuyter and Melyn, accompanied them who had his share of troubles with Kieft and was to answer for charges in Holland. Strangely enough, this would become a very uneventful crossing. Captain Bol had made an error in calculation, mistaking Bristol Channel (or also called the False Channel) for the English Channel and the ship wrecked on 27 September, breaking into pieces against some rocks off Swansea. But just before the wreck, Kieft suddenly had a thought that he needed to express towards Melyn and Kuyter, "Friends," he said, with a sigh, "I have been unjust towards you, can you forgive me?" Of the 100 persons on board, eighty-one passengers were drowned, including Kieft, Bogardus and . . . [25]

> *Cornelis Melyn lost his son. [Bouwen Krynssen, a skipper, answering a conversation to one of his shipmates on an unknown ship, was told by Melyn]*

On the morning of the 28th, off the coast of Mumbles Point, Melyn was nearly lifeless, clinging to a piece of wood. He rode the waves until it tossed him onto a sandbar some two miles from shore. He also found that other passengers had survived and were also making their way ashore. Melyn had found his friend, Kuyter, who was also alive, and had been on the aft part of the ship. It appeared that twenty-one of the 107 passengers had survived the wreck. [26]

> *Melyn floating back to sea, fell in with others who remained upon a part of the ship on a sand bank, which at the ebb-tide became dry,*

*when they took some planks and pieces of wood, which they put together
in the san bar, and took as many shirts and other garments as were
necessary for a sail, so that they were enabled to get from the send bar,
over the channel, to the main-land of England. And these persons were
mostly concerned for their papers, some of which were totally lost on
the sea, they fished for them till the third day.*

*They [Kuyter and Melyn] told me [Bouwen Krynssen, a skipper,
answering a conversation by Charles, a student from Sweden, while
on an unknown ship] afterwards, that when they reached Holland,
they understood the managers lamented very much the loss of the
rich cargo and the ship, and so many fine folks, and grieved that two
bandits, rebels, and mutineers had come to annoy the company with
their complaints.*

Unfortunately Kieft, Bogardus and some of the Company soldiers had died.
Among the ship debris, Melyn and Kuyter were able to salvage a few beaver
pelts and later sold them in a nearby town. These funds were used to make
their way through the rutted, civil-war-scared countryside to Bristol and then
to London in about three weeks later.

When the two arrived in London, they were relying on a colleague, a
Dutch ambassador, Albert Joachimi, to get them home to Holland but was
not available. Both had been stranded in England for months before finally
being able to get into Holland, about late October. Because of the ship wreck,
the waiting to get into Holland basically did nothing of eroding their beliefs
of resolving their issues.

Holland

Melyn wasted no time getting to the States General at The Hague, where
all proceedings against him were eventually suspended. [Bouwen Krynssen,
the skipper of an unknown named ship, was told by Kuyter and Melyn
that . . .] [27]

*. . . some of the managers have attempted to prevent a hearing for them
by their High Mightinesses . . . Van Beeck and Pasquin . . . knew how
to stir up. They obtained a hering, however, and presented their matters
so plainly before their High Mightinesses, that they thought proper to
prohibit such wicked proceedings, dispatching letters of prohibition.*

*They sent for Stuyvesant to come back, or else to send an attorney either
to sustain his sentence, or hear it annulled, or to reverse it there.*

They laid their case before the States General at The Hague, which was
favorably disposed to them. The Directors of the West India Company wrote
to Stuyvesant on 7 April 1648 . . . [28]

*Cornelius Melyn is well known to us, and we shall understand how
to refute his complaint. It is to be regretted that people have become
so intimate with such fellows, when they ought to have given a good
example to others.*

In the office of the Title Guarantee & Trust Company, New York, there is
a painting, done by John Ward Dunsmore, of the departure of the *Princess
Amelia* that left New Netherland on 17 August 1647 for Holland. Out on
the river is seen the waiting ship flying the Dutch flag of the West India
Company. On the shore are assembled two noteworthy groups: on the left,
Peter Stuyvesant, members of his Council, and ex-Director William Kieft.
On the right are the Skipper, Kuyter and Melyn, together with Melyn's young
son . . . [29]

*In the manner and on conditions hereafter expressed the Very Noble
Jongheer (Lord) Godert Van Reede, Lord of Nederhorst, etc., has
agreed with Cornelis Melyn that the said Lord of Nederhorst shall
received and possess in ownership the just half of the colonies acquire
by Cornelis Melyn from the West India Company on Staten Island or
elsewhere to be selected as well in regard to jurisdiction as to ownership
of the lands, woods, and all other rights, appertaining to the said
colony. Which one half said Melyn by these presents cedes to the Lord
of Nederhorst; the other half as well as in regard to jurisdiction,
lands, woods and rights appertaining to the same remaining to the
said Cornelis Melyn; provided that said colony with the consent and
approbation of both parties, shall be divided in two equal parts, an
exact map of which shall be made and sent over by the said Melyn,
to be then drawn for by the said Lord of Nederhorst, and by the said
Melyn. And in case the said Lord of Nederhorst should draw the part
upon which said Melyn should have incurred any expenses, said Lord
of Nederhorst in such case shall pay indemnification, upon the award
of expert arbitrators. With the distinct understanding that each for*

his own share shall bear his own expenses and shall people the same, and further each shall regulate his own property in such a manner as they shall deem proper without having anything further in community with other; with express condition that if the Lord Count of Solms in regard to his Colony should happen to acquire any more privileges from the West India Company or their High Mightinesses, that said Lord of Nederhorst shall also exert himself as much as possible that said Melyn, in such case, shall also receive similar conditions and privileges for his portion, without however being obliged to positively acquire the same. Said Melyn promising to act as superintendent and to take care that the people to be sent there by the Lord of Nederhorst (who will do so soon as his Honor shall find an opportunity) shall be held to the duty, and to act in weighty matters unless with the advice of the said Cornelis Melyn. In ratification of which parties mutually pledge their respective persons and goods, submitting the same for this purpose to all Lords, courts and jurisdictions. In testimony respective parties have subscribed to this present (which remains in the custody of me Jan de Graeff Notary Public at Amsterdam) in the presence of and with me Notary, at Amsterdam, this sixth of May, old style, of the year sixteen hundred forty one. Agrees with the minute of the deceased Notary Jan de Graeff, this 16th January Anno 1648.

By me
F. Steur, Notary Public
1648.
Endorsed:
Agremt with the Lord Nederhorst and Corneli Melyen

On 25 April 1648, the States General granted Melyn and Kuyter a provisional appeal of 28 April where they presented their case. A writ of supersedes or "The Mandamus" was issued to suspend all proceedings from the verdict made by Stuyvesant and his Council. [30]

The States General of the United Netherlands, To the first Marshall or Messenger having power to serve when requested, Greeting: Make Known, that we, having received the humble supplication presented to us by and in behalf of Jochem Pietersz Cuyter and Cornelis Melyn, containing that they, petitioiners, with permission and leave of the Assembly of the XIX of the General West India Company, with wife and children and with private means, besides a large herd of cattle, in the year one thousand six hundred and thirty nine, transported themselves from these countries to New Netherland, so that they, petitioners, after enormous expenses, difficulties and inexpressible labor, got into condition, in the year sixteen hundred forty three, their lands, houses and other undertakings which in the aforesaid year on account of the war (waged by Director Kieft unjustly and contrary to all international law, with the savages or natives of New Netherland) they have been obliged to abandon and as a consequence lost all their property. On account hereof the petitioners, besides the other six Selected Men took counsel and in the name of the joint Commonality in New Netherland in the year sixteen hundred forty four by the Blue Cock, sent two letters: to the said Assembly of the XIX, as also to the Directors in Amsterdam, containing their grievances regarding this matter, the disasters grown out of these actual murders, massacres and many other cruelties (which is appalling to every Christian conscience having information hereof) which Director Kieft at the time, has caused to be perpetrated by his forces among the simple and innocent savages, as may be learned more at large from the original letter to the XIX; so that the Eight selected men did not know that they had transgressed in this matter, but had hoped that the same would have been taken in good part by the Lords Directors. But petitioners find on the contrary that their writings were taken in the worst part by the Lords, who consequently returned said letter with the New Director Stuyvesant to New Netherland to Director Kieft, from which subsequently followed that said Kieft began to proceed very vigorously against the Eight Select Men (especially against both petitioners) and has caused them to be prosecuted by the Fiscal. In such a manner that Director Stuyvesant (in order to please said Kieft in the matter) has banished petitioners for a number of years out of the country because they were not willing to repeal the truth, and adhered to their previous writings. Petitioners thereupon turned to us, requesting, imploring and praying for God's Sake, that we should be pleased to maintain them in their just cause, that they might again be able to join their poor, desolate wives and children, and to be reinstated in their former condition on their devastated lands. And in case petitioners have transgressed through any improper documents (tending to the damage of New Netherland or the common weal, which they have never attempted) they submit to such punishment as we shall find to be proper. But on the contrary it will be shown that petitioners in their writings did not consider anything but that the common prosperity

*and the desire for peace in New Netherland might again be restored,
and that the inhuman cruelties, tyranny and evil government (which in
that country from time to time have been inflicted by the officers of the
West India Company especially by Director Kieft upon the inhabitants
of New Netherland) might be stopped. As a consequence of these barbaric
proceedings the entire government of that country has been erupted
the householders chased away, their lands laid waste, the farms and
plantations to the number of fifty or sixty burnt and reduced to cinders.
And, worst of all, the the name of the Netherland nation, on account of
the cruel acts is most thoroughly detested by the Heathens of that country.
And then when the poor inhabitants complained about these and other
harsh proceedings to the High Sovereign Government, they were, by the
Director, chased out of the country, in such a manner that in course of
time the country was denuded of the Dutch inhabitants, and at present
there are found there little more than a hundred males (excepting the
private traders), and therefore it is to be feared that the English (who
arrived some years after the Dutch, and within fifteen years increased
to about fifty or sixty thousand souls in New England) and already now
have had a taste of the fruitfulness and also of the convenient navigable
rivers of our New Netherland, will in course of time attempt to become
masters of the same. On account whereof petitioners again cordially pray
that this aforesaid, and their humble petitioner may be considered by
us, and they may be granted their reasonable and just request, which
had even been promised by the Assembly of the XIX in their Freedoms of
1630 to all Patroons and Free Residents. Considering which we order
and command you, commissioning you by these presents, that a the
request of the said petitioners you summon in our behalf the aforesaid
Director Stuyvesant and the members of the New Netherland government
before mentioned, besides all others; if necessary to come and appear, or
send attorneys, on an appropriate day, before us here at the Hague, to
maintain and defend the aforesaid sentences and the tenor of the same
or if they deem proper to renounce of the same; to see and to hear the
same pronounced null, void and of no value and in consequence modify
and correct the same, as per law, if such be necessary; to reply to such
questioning as petitioners shall be inclined to put on the proper day, in
order, parties heard, petitioners may be granted by us such remedies of
Justice, and also of grace, if necessary, as shall be found requisite, and be
appropriate to the cause. Further forbidding and most rigorously order in
on our behalf if need be on certain heavy penalty, the aforesaid defendants*

and all others, that pending the case in appeal they do not act, attempt, nor innovate anything against nor in prejudice of the same, nor of the said appellants; but in case anything should have been done, attempted or innovated contrary to the same, that immediately and without delay they repair the same, putting it in its first and proper sate. Leaving, behalf of defendants, copy of the present and of your service, relating to us on the said day what you shall have done in this matter. Given at The Hague, on the twenty eighth of April, sixteen hundred and forty eight.

Hieron: Eyben
By order of the above named Lords States General Corn. Musch 1648

Stuyvesant was summoned to appear before them to justify his acts. Under Dutch rule, this order could be served only by a duly qualified deputy, but since no person was available, an endorsement of 6 May 1648 was made on the mandamus permitting service to be made on Stuyvesant by any person whom Melyn and Kuyter might appoint. They obtained a letter of safety from the Stadholder, William II, Prince Orange (also known as William III, King of England) and would later return to New Amsterdam . . . [31]

The Prince of Orange, Honorable, Prudent, Discreet, Dear Sir: You will receive by the bearers here of Jochem Pietersen Cuyter and Cornelis Melyn, the commands, which their High: Might: the States General have concluded to issue to you, directing you to allow these men to enjoy their property there free and unmolested by virtue of the provisional appeal, granted to them by their High: Might: with the clause suspending the sentence passed over them by you on the 25th of July 1647. Although I do not doubt that you will obey and respect these orders, yet I desire hereby to admonish you earnestly and advise you expressly that you allow these men to enjoy quietly and without contradiction the result of the resolution passed by their High: Might: Herewith, etc., At the Gravens' Hague, May 19th 1648. Your very good friend, w. d'Orange. To the Honorable Prudent, Discreet, Our Dear and Special Friend Petrus Stuyvesant, Director of Netheland.

Endorsed as follows: The States General of the United Netherlands, To all who shall see or hear read this present, greeting Make Known, that having paid attention to the later petition made to us on this day in the name and on behalf of Jochim Pietersz Cuyter and Cornelis

Melyn our subjects, and residents of New Netherland, have amplified, as we are amplifying by the present, the mandamus inscribed on the other side of this present, in such a manner that the said mandamus may be served not only by a messenger, marshall or Notary but by such other person, whether official or private, as the said petitioners, either together or separately, shall be able to acquire and agree upon. Ordering and commanding each and every one whom it may in any way concern, exactly to regulate themselves in conformity herewith, in every appearance as if the aforesaid amplification had been verbally inserted in the aforesaid mandamus. Given in the Hague on the Sixth of May, sixteen hundred forty eight.

J. Van Gent
By order of the above named Lords States General Corn. Musch

It was arranged that Melyn would go back to New Netherland and serve the papers to Stuyvesant, Kuyter would remain in Netherlands to be in readiness if Stuyvesant should act treacherously or arbitrarily. Kuyter eventually made his peace with Stuyvesant, whom with two others he admitted in 1651 into joint ownership with himself in his plantation on the Harlem Flats, where he was actively engaged in restoring his impaired fortunes. But in 1654 he was murdered by the Indians at Harlem.

Voyage 8: 1649, Holland to New Haven and New Netherland

Melyn departed Holland on May of 1649 possibly on the ship *De Jonge Prins van Denmark* (*The Young Prince of Denmark*). Along the way, he had touched some points in New England as Stuyvesant had complained to the States General. In a letter of 10 August of 1649, Stuyvesant states that Melyn "had been running through New England among the English people" showing the documents he had received from the General and that he [Melyn] was empowered to send Stuyvesant to Holland as a prisoner. Melyn arrived in New Haven, Connecticut where he met one of his townsmen, Eghbert van Borsum. After Melyn left, Van Borsum made a deposition of Melyn, " . . . that the High and Mighty Lords, the States of the United Netherlands, were greatly surprised that the English had not forcibly dragged Director Stuyvesant out of the Fort, and hung him on the highest tree; also that he had brought Kieft to his grave and that he would bring Stuyvesant also there." And that he went away, " . . . so that he might no longer listen to the prattle."

He arrived on 1 January 1649 (Kuyter followed later) . . . [32-33]

. . . in New Netherland in front of the Staten Island where, owning to contrary wind and tides, we cast anchor. The people belonging there, joyfully went on land, thanking God for Having been freed from the water and the ship . . . everything began to be abundant on Staten Island, and through God's blessing I began again to recover my losses.

[Bouwen Krynssen, the skipper of an unknown named ship, was told by Kuyter and Melyn that . . .]

. . . And when Cornelis Melyn arrived on the 1st of January, after many hardships, he [Stuyvesant] wanted to take by force all the letters which Melyn had brought with him, to whom he sent the fiscal and secretary twice in the night.

But Melyn sent nothing to him, except the passport of their High Mightinesses. He thereupon sent, the third time, a sergeant to have him appear before the General with his papers. He was answered by Melyn, that he would come before the council in the morning, and then produce and deliver up every thing which he had to produce and deliver. Had it not been for the strong protest of the councilor Lubertus van Dincklage, Vice-Director, who was not willing to have any thing to do with his opposition and hasty rage against the passport of their High Mightinesses, he would with his sailors have thrown Melyn again into prison.

The next day, in the morning, Melyn being summoned, appeared and delivered all the orders and despatches of their High Mightinesses, and also those of His Highness, and of divers others written to him particularly. When these letters were read through, the hand was in the hair [Stuyvesant was perplexed]. Good advice was the best, hwereby he was so far brought over, that he said to Melyn and answered that he, Stuyvesant, would follow the orders of their High Mightinesses, and he, Melyn, should pursue his business as before, But these words had no significance; for Melyn desired to be rung I as he was rung out, and reinstated as a Commonalty's man, from which place he had been unrighteously removed; also to have restitution of the losses he had sustained by these rude and unlawful proceedings. He would grant none of them.

It would be an amazing sight, one day in January of 1649, that Melyn's hometown would see what seemed to have been a ghost that would row itself to the dock. He had written to his compatriots from Bristol explaining the fate of the ship, his and Kuyter's survivorship. Melyn was able to bring with him a writ of mandamus and safe-conduct letter from their High Mightinesses. As soon as he could secure a safe place, he gathered a number of people who considered themselves part of Melyn's political ally's. The Board of Nine eventually read these documents and was surprised. It mentioned that Stuyvesant's sentences against Melyn and Kuyter were both revoked and pending appeal, Stuyvesant, or a representative, was to return to Holland and explain his conduct. And also with this document, Melyn had in his possess a personal letter from Willem, the Prince of Orange . . . [34]

> . . . the war that Director Kieft illegally and contrary to all public Law, had commenced against the Indians . . . which must startle the Christian heart that hears of them.

One of Stuyvesant's plans before actually returning to The Hague was to stall his return by suggesting that the Board of Nine make sure that what they were proposing was the will of the town. Due to the support from Holland the Board decided to follow through. They would ask, one by one, if they felt that the government should be reformed or not. In the process, the Board vacated outside and divided themselves into the streets and began knocking on doors. It appeared that the population had much to say as when they were finished, they compiled a dossier, which Van der Donck collated and distilled the thoughts into a single document.

In the process of interviewing the citizens, Stuyvesant grew angry as to how they could have gone against him. Eventually he couldn't hold his rage any longer and had to let it go. Van der Donck finally had had enough. Somehow he got Stuyvesant to come to his senses and work with the Board. He would work with them and take their advice. Since this would defeat the purpose of the delegation, Van der Donck informed Stuyvesant that the Board . . . [35]

> . . . would not communicate with him or follow his directions in anything pertaining to this matter.

This was the last straw. Stuyvesant ended up exhibiting towards those against him . . . [36]

. . . a bitter and unconquerable hatred but principally against those
whom he supposed to be the chief authors . . .

At this point, Stuyvesant had had enough. He took with him a soldier from
the fort to a member of the Board's home, Michael Janszen. They searched
his home, found and confiscated the documents with the lists of the residents'
complaints, the laments regarding the colony and its management and the
draft that Van der Donck had been working on. Stuyvesant had Van der Donck
arrested the next day and imprisoned. He sent one of his court messengers,
Philip de Truy, to round up the Board of Nine to an "emergency supreme
council." Once the Board had been assembled, Stuyvesant informed them
that Van der Donck's had been arrested and charged with "crirmen laesae
majestatis" (high treason). [37] Suddenly, his vice-director and only lawyer
on the colony, Lubbert van Dinklagen, presented Stuyvesant with a formal
protest, charging that . . . [38]

'. . . the honorable director . . . has theretofore done and still does many
thing "on his own, without informing his council," also because he
has caused Adriaen van der Donck to be placed under arrest 'without
consulting them'

This came as a surprise for Stuyvesant as he was now being accused of being
insubordinate, according to his own council. Stuyvesant collected himself,
changed tactics against Van Dinklagen to where he would read from the
confiscated papers from which Dinklagen defamed the Holland government.
Dinklagen of course denied these writings and demanded to see such pages,
but Stuyvesant refused. Stuyvesant then asked those that were present what
they thought that Stuyvesant should do with Van der Donck. Dinklagen spoke
first insisting that in accordance with Dutch law, Donck should be examined
on the matter and be released on bail. But mostly others agreed with a Brian
Newton, who served Stuyvesant loyally since Curacao, on the notion that he
remain in prison and be interrogated there.

Due to the possibility of Stuyvesant being voted against, he adjourned
the session without calling a vote. A few days later he summoned his council
without the Board and it was decided to keep Van der Donck in custody until
the case was investigated. A few days later, on Monday, 8 March 1649, with
Van der Donck still in confinement, people from all the villages in Manhattan
gathered in the church where Stuyvesant was holding a meeting, Melyn took
advantage of this situation. [39-40]

He now declared in a loud voice his intention to fulfill the wishes of the States General by having the Board of Nine serve the mandamus on Stuyvesant

[Skipper Bouwen Krynssen explains to his shipmates aboard an unknown ship]

It was determined to carry into effect the order of their High Mightinesses on the 8th of March, 1649, at the time when the general, Stuyvesant, had convened the Commonalty of New Netherland in the church, in order that he might have his ample commission read before them, and his sovereign government vindicated thereby. By this he intended to kill dead the present order of their High Mightinesses, or at least to suspend it, besides endeavoring to effect other like designs upon his own responsibility. The vice-director Dincklage protested that he had no knowledge of and gave no consent to these movements, and that the general had of his own motion caused this assembling of the Commanlty, and presented his own views to them without communicating them to him, the vice-director. This protest he villainously ridiculed; whereupon Melyn, perceiving that the longer he staid the worse it was, left the execution of the mandate of their High Mightinesses to be effected by Arnoldus van Hardenberg, who was invited and agreed to do so in presence of the whole Commonalty.

The director-general seeing such unexpected opposition befalling him, did not know what countenance to assume; to attack any one hostilely in the presence of all these witnesses was not prudent, and to do nothing was to injure his reputation before such a large assemblage of more than three hundred persons. He asked Melyn whether he would now let the order be executed, who answered, Yes. He seized the mandate angrily out of the hands of him executing it, so that the seal of their High Mightinesses hung to the parchment in halves, and if it had been paper only, it would have been torn by this irreverent grabbing. When those who stood next to him earnestly admonished him to have respect for their High Mightinesses, a copy of the mandate was placed in his hands by Melyn, and the original mandate was again put in the hand of the person executing it, who read it out loud, and required his answer thereto. Shortly afterwards, the lowest part of the seal fell off.

Melyn later found Arnoldus Van Herdenburg, a member of the Board, and demanded that he read these papers. Stuyvesant knew of these papers, ordered Melyn back to Europe and roared out, "I must have the copy!" [41]

In rage, Stuyvesant snatched the mandamus from Van Herdneburg's hands and in the confusion, the seal was torn off. Melyn then offered Stuyvesant a copy of the mandamus, whereupon the latter was induced by some of the bystanders to return the original, which was read, including the summons commanding Stuyvesant to appear at The Hague to defend the judgment. Stuyvesant could see in front of him that the situation was getting even more out of hand and he knew that he had to do something. The event . . . [42]

> . . . so shaped that massacre and bloodshed might have been the result, had we not converted ourselves from the highest to the lowest, and permitted the indecent service of the summons.

He now realized that he had been trapped by his enemies and in doing so, he brought the assembly to order and directed the men to read the document. Stuyvesant then replied . . . [43]

> I honor the States General, and their Commission, and will obey their Commands, and will send an Agent to maintain the judgment, as it was well and legally pronounced.

After the reading, he left. Melyn demanded a written reply, but it was never given. Stuyvesant refused to give Melyn copies of the sentence and other papers in the case. The safe conduct from William of Orange was passed by Stuyvesant's Council with a resolution "in obedience to orders from the States General and the Prince of Orange" permitting Melyn to reside in New Netherland. On 29 July 1649, Melyn protested against Stuyvesant, of 9 August . . . [44]

> It is now about seven months since I arrived here with their High MIghtinesses' Mandamus and Order, which, on the 8th March, were served on you Petrus Stuyvesant, Director, and afterwards on the other members of the Court. Accordingly on the twentieth on March I demanded reintegration, pursuant to the tenor of the Mandamus, and observing neglect, on the 20th June, insisted and at divers times applied verbally, for the most part, in these terms—Pursuant to the Mandamus and your obligation to honor their High Mightinesses and

their Commission (I demand) reintegration and such satisfaction as that brings with it; I have now borne long enough with postponement and fruitless promises; time is short and the vessels are making ready; if your Honor designs to make restitution or reparation, let it be done quickly, according to the tenor of the Mandamus; if not, I herebyt protest against you.

And if your Honor intends to maintain what, if you have yet any conscience left, you cannot deny to be your Honro's pronounced sentence, you must appear personally, or by another qualified to represent you and will so stand and suffer and bear what is charged against you, as if you were yourself there; you shall also permit the other member of the court, who is subject to you, to depart in person, or some other individual for him; for one delinquent cannot defend the other; and in case such be not done, I do hereby again protest.

I demand, according to your Honor's promise, that all copies both of judgment, affidavits, acts and proceedings which have been heretofore refused, be seasonably furnished me, in order that I may also summon the deponents, for the affidavits which Myn heer, or his like, take here from their subjects, who must say what you please, are, I my opinion of no value, and, as I, therefore, conclude, of no force in law. In case, then, all the documents, proceedings and declarations, or one or any of them, which are to be used in law against me, are detained from me; and in case they are refused me, and copies of the papers and documents are not furnished, as heretofore has been the case, I declare that I am deprived of, and excluded from the right and proper means of justice and legal evidence, against rules and order to you well known.

In like manner I do declare null, void, and of no effect all acts, proceedings, affidavits and declarations whereof I have not obtained copies here, and of which use shall hereafter be made against me, being utterly unworthy of consideration of account of the suspicion of being acknowledged I bad faith; and, thirdly, against you, Petrus Stuyvesant, Director, individually, and against all the members of the Court generally, do I protest for and on account of all damage and losses already suffered or yet to arise, from the omission and neglect of orders and instructions to do what is right; and their High Mightinesses command and expressly order you, in case you do not repent, to wit, sincerely and indeed, and not in fine phrases, as has hitherto been your case.

Dated Manahatans, New Netherland, this 29ᵗʰ July, 1649.
(Signed)

Stuyvesant answered to this protest . . . [45]

We hear and see, but protest against the disrespectful discourtesies contained in the protest, especially against the seditious service of the Mandamus, at an unsuitable place, in the Church, and with much disparaging language in presence of the entire Commonalty. Nevertheless, we esteem the service valid, and say, as before, that we shall honor and regard whatever our Sovereigns will decide. We are no ways bound to restitution, since we have not received anything; nor to any reparation so long as the case is in appeal, and no additional injury done the protestor. We grant and allow him peaceable use of his lands and effects; what I have promised I shall perform; namely, to send an Attorney to hear, and to witness the confirmation or annulment; what other officers, councilors, will do, whether to go to stay, we leave at their discretion and pleasure. Therein we have nothing to command; neither does it quadrate with the tenor of the Mandamus.

Who the delinquent is, God and the law have to decide. The protestor has never been refused copy of the judgment. The party must apply for the other papers in the suit and appear before the Judge who will have prudence and knowledge enough to decide what and which affidavits ought to be produced; whether they have been legally taken before Commissioners or whether they were given clandestinely and by inducement to affront and asperse the Judge, on which points the opinion of the protestor himself is of no avail. Of damage and losses we deem ourselves guiltless, since we do not oblige the protestor to pay any costs, or the return anew to Fatherland. We give and grant him, pending the matter in appeal, the quiet possession and peaceable use of his lands, houses and property.

Done Manhattans this 1ˢᵗ August, 1649 (Signed) P. Stuyvesant.

This document of 10 August 1649: [46]

> *. . . in which he for a great part receded from his former sentence, especially from the banishment; excusing himself also that he was not bound to make restitution because he had received nothing, and also because he understood that while the matter was hanging under appeal he was not obliged to make restitution, and alleging similar frivolous reasons; and leaving Melyn in free possession of his goods and effects. In short, of all what this affrighted judge had undertaken, his troubled conscience remained. Seeing that the men stood firm to their purpose, that he should either make them reparation or send an attorney to Holland, he resolved to send the Secretary Tienhoven to Holland; and in order that he might anticipate then, the secretary went in a small ship fourteen days before them, and we, with the deputies of the Commonalty, followed fourteen days afterwards. But as the secretary ran behind Ireland, as he deemed it necessary to do so, in order not to get on the same shoal as Kief, ans as we, with the deputies of the Commanlty, took our course straight to the Channel, we got in before him.*

Encouraged by the results of Melyn and Kuyter's efforts, a jurist, Adriaen van der Donck, prepared a historical document, "The Remonstrance of New Netherland" [July 1649]. It attacked the whole policy of the West India Company in relation to its colony of New Netherland and would be sent to Holland with Van der Donck, Melyn and Stuyvesant's Secretary, Van Tienhoven.

Voyage 9: 1649, New Netherland to Holland

Melyn departed New Netherlands with the historical documents for the prosecution of the appeal about 24 August 1649 possibly on the ship *Prins Willem*, arriving in Holland on 4 October 1649. In this document, some of its signers were leading burghers of New Amsterdam . . . [47]

> *In the proceedings against Cuyter and Melyn every one saw that Director Kieft had more favor and aid and counsel in his suit than his adversary and that one Director was the advocate of the other as Director Stuyvesant's own words imported and signified when he said, 'These Boorish Brutes would hereafter endeavor to knock me over also, but I shall now manage it so that they will have their bellies full for all time to come . . .' When Melyn pleaded for race until the result of his appeal to Fatherland, he was threatened in these words, 'Had I known,*

Melyn, that you would have divulged our sentence or brought it before their Mightinesses, I should have had you hanged forthwith on the highest tree in New Netherland . . .' On another occasion Stuyvesant said, 'People may think of appealing in my time, should any do so, I would have him made a foot shourter, pack the pieces off to Holland, and let him appeal in that way.

Stuyvesant sent Secretary Van Tienhoven to Holland to defend the sentence and on 26 November 1649, he presented Stuyvesant's answer [dated 10 August 1649]. Van Tienhoven took another vessel on the long route "back to Ireland" to avoid the fate of the *Princess*, so that it and *Prins Willem* would arrive on the same day in Holland, 4 October 1649. Here, Stuyvesant's secretary and Melyn left together. Melyn's protector, Godard van Reede, had died and the case was shuttled back and forth between the States General and the Company and so no clear-cut decision was ever obtained. After Melyn left, his son-in-law, Captain Loper, applied for permission to trade in the South or Delaware River, but although the council was in favor of granting the application, Stuyvesant refused, only replying that he had received express orders from his superiors "to keep an eye on Cornelis Melyn." Melyn's wife had written him on 17 December [1649], "We wish that God would be pleased to send the delegates back quickly, with business accomplished, for here matters continue so bad as to excite murmurs against Heaven . . . poor people have scarcely enough to eat, for no supplies of bread, butter, beef and pork can now be had, except for beaver or silver coins." The letter went on to say Stuyvesant, "promised the people either beavers or silver coin, or cargoes in the spring." She ended the letter with a final descriptive sentence of the hardships endured in the new land. "It is so cold here, that the ink freezes in the pen." Melyn appeared to become wearied due to the delays of the Council's decision, since on 8 February 1650, he complained to them that he was unable to obtain certain papers needed for his suit and that he suggest the Council take consideration that he . . . [48-49]

> *. . . hath now groped such a length of time, since the year 1643, in this labyrinth, without any error or fault of his, for the advancement of the public interests.*

> *. . . being in the meanwhile obliged to neglect for so long a time his private affairs and family (being burdened with six children) and to encounter to his excessive cost and great injury, all sorts of vexation*

and trouble in his private affairs, on account of a public matter so entirely just.

On 8 February 1650, Melyn addressed to the States General this petition . . . [50]

To the High and Mighty Lords the Lords States General of the United Netherlands. High and Mighty Lords!

Cornelis Melyn, Patroon on Staten Island in New Netherland, your High Mightinesses' humble servant, respectfully showeth: That he repaird to New Netherland with your High Mightinesses; Mandamus in case of appeal and favorable letter, obtained herein the year 1648, against the sentence pronounced by Director Petrus Stuyvesnat and his Council, on your Petitioner, and caused due service of said Mandamus on the abovenamed Director and his Council, as well as on all others in any wise concerned, pursuant to the tenor of your High Mightinesses' addition endorsed on the aforesaid Mandamus. Petrus Stuyvesand, the Director, treated the service of the Mandamus with very boisterous dis-respect, tearing it in the presence of all the People, out of the officer's hands, so that your Hight Mightinesses' own seal fell off, and had the Mandamus not been written on parchment but only paper, it would indeed have been torn in pieces; all of which will further appear by the return of the officer in the copy hereunto annexed, the original whereof is in Petitioner's possession. And notwithstanding the Petitioner hath not been able to obtain, either before or after judgment, nor even after service was made of your High Mightinesses' andamus, nor after his indispensable protest, aught or any of the papers and documents against him whereby the judgment is claimed to be well sustained, nor sufficient copies thereof; notwithstanding the declaration of Vice-Director Lubbertus Van Dinclagen, a Doctor of Law, as by the return can be seen, that he (the petitioner) is wronged by Director Petrus Stuyvesant and his advisors detaining the papers which are favorable to the petitioner, and otherwise apply to the vote on the judgment; notwithstanding also, that Henrick Opdyck, the fiscal, in answer to the petitioner, denied being a party in the suit against him, and other councilors offer other excudes and subterfuges yet he, your petitioner, cannot obtain in fairness from Director Stuyvesant, according to the tenor of the abovementioned Mandamus, any revocation of the judgment, nor reparation of suffered defamation and loss; but inasmuch as the aforementioned Director, about fourteen days previous to your petitioner's last departure from New Netherland, did dispatch hither his Secretary, Cornelis van Tienhoven, who, when summoned, obstinately refused to answer on service of your High Mightinesses' Mandamus, your petitioner hath finally found himself obliged immediately to follow him.

Therefore, in order to complain of the abovementioned frivolous, unfounded judgment, as well as to institute his further action which he hath against the abovenamed Secretary, the petitioner humbly applies to your High Mightinesses, respectfully requesting that you would be pleased to appoint time and place for the said Secretary to appear and to hear such demand and conclusion as your petitioner shall make against him as principal, and as attorney, as the same shall then be found requisite.

Wherefore the petitioner, most respectfully, and with all humility, prays that your High Mightinesses will be pleased to help him, for once, to the speedy expedition of his good right, and to take into consideration that your petitioner hath now groped such a length of time, since the year 1643, in this labyrinth without any error or fault of his, for the advancement of the public interests, being, in the meanwhile, obliged to neglect, for so long a time, his private affairs and family, being burdened with six children, and to encounter, to his excessive cost and great injury, all sorts of vexation and trouble in his private affairs, on account of a public matter so entirely just; therefore the petitioner will respectfully expect your High Mightinesses; favorable postil and speedy conclusion, inasmuch as the time for returning back draws nigh. Which doing, &c.

(In the margin was:)

The States General of the United Netherlands have, upon previous deliberation, placed this petitioner, with the papers annexed, in the hands of Messrs. Van Aartsbergen and other their High Mightinesses' Deputies for the West India Company's affairs, to inspect and to examine them, and to hear and understand the petitioner and Secretary Van Tienhoven who is at present here at the Hague, again and again, and

*to make a report on the whole manner to their High Mightinesses Done
at the Assembly of the Noble States General, the 8th February, 1650.*

*(Signed) Johan Van Reede, VT.
By order of the same
(Endorsed) Cornelis Melyn.
(Signed) Corns Musch, 1650.*

Records are suggested to exist but don't show what the end result was. Melyn and Kuyter were both now anxious to return to New Netherland now that the Indian attacks had subsided and needing to restore their plantations. With Melyn's long sojourn at The Hague, he was in contact with many government officials, one being the Baron van der Capellen, which had taken an interest in Melyn's affairs. Van der Capellen wrote a report concerning this to the Committee and then entered into an agreement to help in the improvement of Melyn's State Island manor. Melyn had gained the support of Baron Henryk van der Capellen, a deputy to the States General and of independent fortune, in his colonization scheme that on 4 June 1650 he sold him an interest in Staten Island in improving and developing his manor. This agreement recited that the Lord of Nederhortst, who had been the owner of a one-half interest in the project, had agreed shortly before his death in 1648, to a division of the property. Van der Capellen, Nederhorst and Melyn were each to then become the owner of a one-third interest, subject to certain conditions. This agreement, of 4 June 1650, was merely the formal completion of the transaction, as Van der Capellen and others, had on 18 May 1650, purchased in the *Nieuw Nederlandtsche Fortuyn* (*New Netherland's Fortune*) and prepared it for its voyage to New Netherland. On 9 June 1650, Melyn appointed a Power of Attorney at The Hague constituting Johannes Grevinck as his general attorney in all his affairs, and his special attorney "together with one or more attorneys, as he shall see fit." On 30 June 1650, Melyn received a safe conduct from the States General, the same as before, against Stuyvesant . . . [51]

Letter of Protection and Safeguard for Cornelis Melyn, Patroon and Colonist on Staten Island in New Netherland, permitting him to return thither.

The States General of the United Netherlands. To all those who shall see these or hear them read. BE IT KNOWN: That We have granted on the 28th April 1648, unto Cornelis Melyn, Patroon and Colonist on Staten Island in New Netherland, provision of appeal, with inhibitory clause from the sentence which was pronounced against him by Peter Stuyvesant, Director of New Netherland under the jurisdiction of the West India Company, with the advice of his Council, on the 25th July of the year 1647. And whereas the aforesaid suit is not yet terminated and the actual circumstances of the petitioner do not by any means admit of his longer sojourn in this country, Therefore, We, after previous deliberation, have granted and accorded, as We do hereby grant and accord unto him, safe conduct and passport to repair freely from thes country back against to New Netherland aforesaid, the abovementioned suit notwithstanding; and he shall be accordingly at liberty to dwell there on his property unmolested and undisturbed by any person whatsoever, during the time that the suit remains here undecided; the petitioner having empowered a person here to defend his right in or out of court against the said sentence. Wherefore We order and command all and every person being in our service and under our obedience, whom this may in any wise concern, either in this country, on the passage, or in New Netherland, and especially the abovenamed Stuyvesant and his Council that they shall cause and allow the abovenamed petitioned to enjoy the full effect hereof, and accordingly, not to molest him in his person nor in any wise to be hindering unto him, on pain of incurring our highest indignation. Given at the Hague under our seal, paraph and signature of our Secretary, the 30th June XVIc and fifty.

Voyage 10: 1650, Holland to New Netherland and Staten Island

Although his case was seemingly never settled, Melyn departed about 10 August 1650 to America on the ship *Nieuw Nederlandtsche Fortuyn* as he brought more colonists with him. The boisterous sea had delayed the ship causing "water had fallen short," and the "last biscuit been divided among the passengers." The ship's captain was obliged to stop at Rhode Island to replenish supplies.

Melyn arrested

Melyn had planned to recoup some of his financial losses once he would return back to New Netherland, but unfortunately, he would run into troubles with Stuyvesant for taking his ship off course. At sunset, about 19

December 1650, on the day the ship arrived in Staten Island, Stuyvesant's soldiers came abroad to prevent Melyn and his colonists from unloading and selling any goods, without paying duty, assuming that Melyn was its real owner. Stuyvesant was always on the lookout for anything that might put Melyn into the clutches of the law. Van Dincklagen investigated the cause of the delayed trip back to New Netherlands. Due to this deviation of the ship's course, Stuyvesant seized this opportunity as a violation of the Company's regulation forbidding the breaking of bulk en route to New Netherland, and caused legal proceedings against Melyn as part owner of the ship and cargo. He was ordered to command his crew to hoist anchor and sail up to Manhattan. Stuyvesant accused Melyn of unloading and selling cargo in Rhode Island for his private gain, thereby "defying and disobeying the rules and instructions of the Company." On 22 April 1651, Stuyvesant confiscated about two-thirds of Melyn's property, dividing it into four lots and selling it to various people, one being his Secretary, Cornelis van Tienhoven. The crew and Melyn were arrested and thrown into prison on 22 August 1651. The ship and goods were confiscated and Stuyvesant proceeded to sell Melyn's house and land on Manhattan. As Melyn could not be found to have had any interest in the ship, the action against him fell through. But new proceedings were begun against the skipper and the ship and therefore, its cargo was condemned and sold. This caused great expense to the West India Company and was later compelled to make restitution to Van der Capellen and his associates. Van der Capellen sued the Company for illegal seizure of his ship and was awarded heavy damages. The confiscation of the *Fortuyn*, her cargo and the consequent inability of Melyn and Van Der Capellen to retain the people brought over in her were a severe blow to their plans. Stuyvesant filed more charges against Melyn and therefore summoned him to Fort Amsterdam to answer to them. Melyn refused to go and his remaining property on Manhattan Island was confiscated and sold by the government. Expecting that an attempt would be made to arrest him, he fortified his manor house on one of the hills overlooking the present village of Clifton. Between the lot of Sibout Claessen (south side of Hoogh Straet, which was immediately west of Melyn's second house) and the Town House, upon the south side of the High Street, lay the confiscated land of Cornelis Melyn. Portions of Melyn's estate not taken was divided into four parcels extending from "the road," or the present Stone Street, to the river shore, and these were granted to various people in September 1651. Because his wife and children pleaded for his release, Melyn was released following the Indian attack on Manhattan and went directly to Staten Island. He tried to reattempt colonization on the

Island but "the Director began by manifesting his old hatred and partisanship" and appeared that his work would have to be abandoned. But Melyn was able to get things back in order "so that everything began to be abundant on Staten Island, and through God's blessing I again began to recover my losses." Melyn continued living for several years in Staten Island. A very interesting letter (No. 4 of the Dodd and Livingston Collection) of 25 June 1652, with his autograph and signatures of six other early settlers of the Island, states that Director Stuyvesant had hired Indians to rob and kill people on Staten Island. It also stated that Melyn was living on the Island at that time and was still having trouble with Stuyvesant.

There are many court transactions that had involved Cornelius in the meantime . . . [52-60]

> *(13 April 1654), Mr. Arent van Hattem reported to the Court that, pursuant to the order of Burgomaster and Schepens, he had an interview with the Honorable General, who said, that the proposition was entirely agreeable to him and that he was well inclined to assist in bringing this City into a state of defense, and for that purpose appointed Friday or Saturday following, to go in person around and speak to the outside people on this subject. But nothing of this had been done. Also, that his Honor would speak or write to Cornelis Melyn of Staten Island about it, who had said some time ago that he was ready to lend a helping hand.*

> *(26 October 1654), Pieter Schaelbank, pltf, v/s Cornelis Melyn, deft., states, that Cornelis Melyn made an assignment on 15 Sept. in favor of Yonkher Reychout van Fruyl to receive in Holland fl. 362. 14., which as per acc't. belonged to him. And as the same was not paid, he requests that the same be paid here with interest @ 12 per cent. Per annum. Dirk Schelluyne appears for Cornelis Melyn, and denies neither the hand writing nor debt. But requests, that pltf. Shall declare, under Oath, that no satisfaction was given, nor anything received in Holland. Pltf. Offers to give sufficient security to repay the money without loss or damage, if deft. Can prove, that it was received in Holland. The Court of the City of New Amsterdam condemns deft. To pay pltf, within one month the aforesaid fl. 362. 14. With interest at 10 per cent. Per an., provided pltf. Pieter Schaefbanck, shall give good and sufficient security according to the aforesaid proposal.*

(15 March 1655), Cornelis Melyn, pltf. v/s Lubbert van Dincklager, deft., demands payment of fl. 300 according to obligation dated 4 Jan 1651, drawn by L. van Dincklagen and Jacob Loper in favor of Augustine Heermans, and assigned to Schrick and conveyed again by Schrick to Cornelis Melyn. Deft. Requires, that pltf. shall institute his action in writing, but acknowledges, that he signed the obligation with Jacob Loper. Burgomasters and Schepens condems deft. Lubbert van Dincklagen to pay as his part the sum of fl. 150, being half of the note, and decides, that Cornelis Melyn shall prove, who owes the other half.

(31 May 1655), Cornelis Melyn, pltf. v/s Sybout Claesen, deft. Deft. In default. Jahan de Decker appeared in Court as attorney for pltf. and handed in his demand and conclusion, but inasmuch as deft, is absent, default is granted.

(7 June 1655), Cornelis Melyn, pltf. v/s Sybout Clasen deft. Johan de Decker, attorney for pltf. being absent and the copy of the demand delivered in last Court day by him, being handed to deft., he excepts thereto, that the demand and conclusion are not signed by Cornelis Melyn, and says the lot is question is almost pad for, Deft. Sybout Clasen, was ordered by the Court to answer in writing by the next Court dday to the demand and to prove what he has paid.

(14 June 1655), Sybout Clasen, deft. In the case of Cornelis Melyn pltf. delivers in his answer or exception to the demand, in writing to the Court, pursuant to the order to settle, being content, that deft. Shall deduct from his promised monies, what he shall legally prove to have paid. Ordered by the Court, that DeDecker as attorney for Cornelis Melyn shall be granted copy of the remarks delivered in by Sybout Clasen, so as to communicate in writing to the Court whatever he, DeDecker, can allege thereon.

(21 June 1655), Johan de Decker as attorney of Cornelis Melyn delivers a certain writing against Sybout Claeseen to the Court, whereupon was endorsed: Copy here of shall be furnished to the party to answer thereunto by the next Court day.

(28 June 1655), Sybout Claessen answers in writing to the document delivered last Monday to the Court by Johan de Decker as attorney for

Cornelis Melyn, whereon was endorsed: Ordered by the Court, that Copy hereof shall be granted the party to reply thereto.

(5 July 1655), Cornelis Melyn serving reply to the answer of Sybout Claesen, thereupon was endorsed-Copy hereof shall be delivered to party thereunto to rejoin by the next Court day.

Unaware of what was going on in Manhattan, Melyn went there in August 1655 in order to transact some business. During this time, Stuyvesant was engaged in conquesting the Swedish colony on the Delaware, and in the process, accused Melyn of encouraging and arranging an attack by some of the Swedes. When Melyn arrived, Stuyvesant met him with a guard of soldiers. Melyn was arrested and "thrown in a dark hold" for 25 days until the outbreak of what was to come, the Peach War. On 31 August 1655, Melyn's wife asked that he be removed to a more convenient place, "on account of his sore leg." The Council made an order that she might be permitted to remove him to a more convenient place, "in the City Hall, or elsewhere," on condition that he should furnish bail. He was still there early in September when Stuyvesant and seven hundred men in seven vessels sailed out of harbor for the Delaware River, where they broke up certain Swedish settlements.

Peach War

One fall day in 1655, a man named Hendrick Van Dyke, who lived on Manhattan Island, looked out his window and saw an Indian woman take a peach from a tree in his garden. He shot her. Soon, Dutch settlers found they had 200 angry warriors tearing the Island apart looking for the culprit. They eventually found and seriously wounded him. After deaths to both sides, the warriors retired across the Hudson and burned Dutch farms at Pavonia, Hoboken and Staten Island. This became the Peach War. When the attack began, Melyn had been let out of his cell and he hastened to the Island where he witnessed the destruction of his colony. It appears that Melyn returned to the Island on 15 September 1655 as he witnessed the burning of the buildings by the Indians. The Indians broke through the palisade around Melyn's large house where he and his family and other colonist had prepared for the siege. The Indians had set fire to the wooden roof. Melyn wrote that when the cinders began to fall, they were obliged to leave and break through the Indians to run down to a smaller house on the shore. One of Melyn's sons, a son-in-law and two nephews were killed in that rush into the open. The survivors reached their refuge and barricaded themselves inside, hoping and praying that help would come from Manhattan, but none came. Finally, the small house was set on fire and Melyn was faced with the terrible alternative of allowing his people to be burned alive or surrendering to the Indians and facing probably torture. He chose to take the risk, offering the Indians ransom if his were released unharmed. They were taken prisoner but not tortured. Fifty persons were captured and held for 31 days while negotiations were being made between the Indians and Melyn's friends on Manhattan. Finally the ransom money, about 1400 guilders, was brought across the river. Melyn, his family, and the other colonists were released. According to Melyn, the ransom "was to be paid if we did not want to be burnt alive in a fire which for this purpose had been already prepared and was burning." They were taken to Manhattan and hoped for some "quiet after their sad imprisonment." The next day, soldiers with firearms and swords informed Melyn that Stuyvesant had claimed that the Indians demanded further ransom, forced him to pay 60 or 70 guilders more, or else be returned to his former prison, the "dark hole." For Melyn, this was the end of his efforts. Due to the destruction of his colony and the continued persecution by Stuyvesant, Melyn decided "for the time being, to put myself under the protection of the English." He gave up his patroonship and left Staten Island and moved to New Haven, Connecticut.

Here are a few court transactions that involves his wife, Janneken . . . [61-63]

(29 November 1655), Jannetie Melyns, pltf. v/s Capt. Pos, deft. Deft, in default.

(6 December 1655), Jannetie Melyn appeared in Court complaining against Andries Pos for alienating and making away with her property. The Complainant was ordered by the Court to enter he complaint duly writing, when it shall be disposed of.

(13 December 1655), Jannetie Melyns, pltf. v/s Capt. Andries Pos, deft. Relative to difference about certain cattle, which pltf. has on Staten Island and which deft. Prevents her bringing hither; and also that deft. Appropriates, what pltf. still owns there, whereby she suffers great damage. Whereas circumstances do not admit fully to establish the matter in question with proof of what the parties allege, the Burgomaster and Schepens have referred the case in dispute between parties to two impartial Arbitrators, whereunto were requested and commissioned

Sieurs Paulus Leendertsen Van die Grift and Givert Loockermans, who are hereby authorized to decided the difference of parties, after consider proper, but it they cannot reconcile parties, they shall report in writing their opinion of the case to the Board. Done as above.

New Haven, Connecticut, Oath of Fidelity

In 1656, Melyn and his son Jacob went to New Haven, Connecticut since it was the closest English town and that he knew a number of the Dutch merchants. According to Court Records of New Amsterdam of 28 February 1656, a fragment of an original Power of Attorney from Janneken's son-in-law, Jacob Schellinger, of 6 April 1656, among the Melyn papers, seem to indicate the approximate time of the removal of the Melyn family from New Amsterdam to New Haven . . . [64]

[One line entirely destroyed] . . . Melyn on her departure . . . declared to constitute and [half a line out] her son in law Jacob Schellinger . . . to, in her prospective absence, the cattle [out] her . . . are on the Staten Island, to have them as early as possible ferried across, and to sell the same to her largest profit, to pay the debts resting on the same, as well to Andries POS, as those incurred in conveying the same and other expenses, and as quickly as possible to send over the balance as per verbal orders given concerning the same; and further generally in the above case, to act and do in everything as she, the principal or her husband himself, if present should and might do, even if further or more specific power might be required than is here expressed. Promising to consider and to have considered valid, binding and well done what her aforesaid attorney shall have done and executed in the aforesaid matter. Binding her person and goods, provided that the attorney, under equal bond, be held upon request to render account, proof and reliqua of his receipts and disbursements. Thus granted and passed in the presence of Casper Steymets and Isaack KIP, as witnesses invited this April 6th 1656, at Amsterdam in New Netherlands.

Janneken Melyen
Witnesses
Caper Steinmets
Isack KIP
Known to me
Jacob KIP, Secretary

The earliest reference of Melyn being in New Haven is of 11 February 1655, when "Mr. Muloine," among others, was assigned one of the "long seats in the middle for the men."

More court transactions involving Janneken . . . [65-68]

> *(17 January 1656), Adraen Keyser, pltf. v/s Jannetie Melyns, deft. Deft. In default.*

> *(28 February 1656), Tryntie van Hengelen, pltf. v/s Jannetie Melyns, deft. Pltf. demands, that deft. Shall account to and settle with her for what belongs to her. Cornelia Schellinger, as security and attorney for deft., her mother, answers that the mother has not the acct. here, but at the North. Requests delay until her return, being shortly. The Court grants deft. Her request.*

> *Cornelia Schellinger, pltf. v/s Adriaen Keyser, deft. Pltf. demands, as on 17th of last January, payment of fl. 30. 2. Deft. Acknowledges the debt as before. And whereas the deft. Remains in default, n the order of 17 January aforesaid, to shew, tht Jannetie Melyn had accepted to meet the abovementioned fl. 30. 2. The Court condemns deft. Adriaen Keyser to pay pltf. Within 8 days.*

> *(24 April 1656), Tryntie van Hengelen, pltf. v/s Jannekie Melyns, deft. Pltf. in default. Jacob Schellinger appears in place of deft., his mother in law, who is absent. Ordered to settle with each other without longer delay.*

On 14 June 1656, the Directors of the Company wrote Stuyvesant asking him to have a thorough search made of all items relating to Staten Island, and to dispatch them to Amsterdam as soon as possible. They then added . . . [69-70]

> *Look out meanwhile, that Cornelis Melyn, who we understand is now at the North, and in negotiation about the [Staten] Island, does not sell or deliver it to a foreign nation, not subject to our jurisdiction; in such a case you must seize it for the Company, as having the best title, and endeavor cautiously to inveigle said Melyn to New Amsterdam, arrest and keep him, and then send him well treated but also well secured, to this country, if the above rumor proves to be true.*

(30 October 1656), Tryntie van Hengelen, pltf. v/s Cornelia Schellingers as att'y for her mother, Jannetie Melyns, deft. For difference of a/c and arrest of an ox, demanding fl. 166. Parties being heard, are referred by the court to two arbitrators, to wit, Dirk van Schelluyn and Hendrick Jansen Vin, to settle the a'cs of parties in dispute before Cornelia Schellinger's departure. Meanwhile the arrest of the ox was again declared valid.

There have been a number of interesting complaints made at a Court on 4 December 1656. First, "That the Duchmen lately admitted doe sell things excessive deare" in support of which there was exhibited a knot of small silk buttons that were priced to sell at 18d a dozen. Second, "That the mault house is not improved, as Mr. Melyn promised it should, to supply the Towne." Third, "That they [the 'Dutchmen'] doe not attend the publique meetings on the Lord's day soe duly as they should." About which, "the Court, with Mr. Davenport, the decons and Townsmen were desired to meete this afternoon and speake with them, that so what is offensive may be removed." The result of this meeting is not recorded. From Court records, on 17 August 1657, Melyn subscribed 10 shillings, apparently for a charitable purpose, which was the largest subscription of four recorded. [71] It would appear that Melyn did hear of this and could have caused him to take the Oath of "fidellitee ye 2 mo 1657."

Widening the Ditch, Manhattan

After the Indian troubles of 1655 had somewhat subsided, it was decided to open up and to regulate several streets, in order to afford accommodation to the increasing number of those who desire to build in the town. One of the changes proposed in the early part of 1656 was to widen and deepen "The Ditch," so as to form a canal navigable for small boats, with a sufficient roadway on each side of it. In 1657, the authorities decided to change the ditch in Broad Street into a graft, the Heere Graft, or canal, with a roadway on each side. As a result, Melyn's property would have to be taken. In June of 1656, Jacob Schellinger, Melyn's son-in-law, was notified not to proceed with the rest of his immediate neighbors in the construction of sheet-piling along their water-fronts, "as his house lies in the canal and on the road." Desiring to control more landing this vicinity than his original small plot, in August 1644, he bought from the widow of Eben Redeenhaus, for the sum of 150 guilders, or about $100, per house and ground. In December of that year, he bought from Burger Jorissen, his house and a larger parcelf of 950 guilders, or $380, he now owned all the land along the river from "the Ditch" to the City Tavern. A year or two after, his house was demolished. In partial compensation, the Burgomaster gave the Melyn's a lot of only 18 feet square at the southeast corner of Hoogh Straet (present Stone Street) and the Graft. This lot had been gained by the straightening of Hoogh Straet which took place about this time, the western end of that street being shifted some 20 or 25 feet northwards, in order to make it connect more nearly with Brouwer Straet (present Stone Street, west of Broad). This is where the second Melyn house was built. The house had nominally belonged to the infant children of Captain Jacob Loper of Cornelia Melyn, but would soon pass into the other members of the family.

More Court transactions involving Janneken . . . [72-73]

> *(20 May 1658), Pieter Jacobzen Marius, ltf. v/s Jenneke Melein, deft. Pltf. demenads from deft. Fl. 204: 3 for a/c of Jan Janse, cheesemonger, as her attorney. Deft. Answers, she recorded 3 @ 400 guilders in loose sewant from Jan Jansen; demanding what she disbursed for him and that she paid something now and again on it and had settled with him before he left, and afterwards paid something on it, so that there remains fl. 30. The Court refer the matter in question to Jacobus Vis and Joannes Withart to decide the a/c and to reconcile parties if possible; otherwise to report to the Court.*

> *(20 August 1658), Jannetie Meleins, ltf. v/s Sibout Clasen, deft. Pltf. demands from deft. Payment of a lot. Pltf. is asked, if she has authority from her husband? Answers, No. Schepen Cornelis Steenwyck exhibits in Court certain Acteof arbitration rendered by him and Govert Loockermans regarding the case in question between Sibout Clasen and Jannetie Meleins, which award is approved by the Court. Deft. Says, he has not received a deed of the lot; and as Jannetie Melein has not any power from her husband, no disposition can be made in the case.*

Voyage 11: 1658, New Netherland to Holland

Sometime before December 1658, Melyn and his two sons, Jacob and Isaac, departed New Netherlands on an unknown named ship. [74]

> *Cornelius Melyen at ye desire of the Lords of the West India company at their chamber in Amsterdam, declares what he knows concerning*

*ye purchase of Staten Island from the Indians in New-Netherland,
& what they receiv'd for ye payment of it, Sayith that Anno 1640.
(at which time ye aforesd. Lords had granted him License to plant &
manure his sd. Colony of Staten Island) he went to ye late Governr
Walter Vantwilder (then being at Amsterdam) of whom he amongst
other things Enquired into ye circumstance of ye purchace of Staten
Island of ye Indians, who answered him, that ye Island was bought &
paid for by ye Governr Minnewit, who immediately preceded him; He
desired him (if he could) to do him ye kindness of furnishing him with
ye relation thereof in writing, wch (at his request) he did, & gave him
some days after a written Copy taken out of ye purchac'd deed (or bill
of Sale) which shew'd what pay ye Indians receiv'd for sd, Island, vizt.
Some Duffies Kittles, Axes, Hoes, Wampum, Drilling Awls, Jews Harps,
and diverse other small wares, which were all particularizd, wch Bill
of Sale was signed by diverse Indians & remaind I his custody intill ye
Dunkirkers took him, his Ship, people, Cattle & all his writings—The
Year following arriving in New Netherland & being come on Staten
Island I (ye sd. Cornelius Melyen) caused ye Indians to be askt whether
they were not well recompenced by Minnewit for sd. Island, They gave
me for Answer, yt they had sold it to sd. Minnewit & were paid for
it, but that it was their custome, when New Governr came to such a
place, that there should be a Gratuity given them; thereby to continue
the friendship between ye Indians & o nation, which I did to ye great
content & Satisfaction of them all—After this when I took out my
Patent from Gover Willm Kieft pursuant to ye grant of ye aforesd. Lords,
I desired that ye Indians might once again be ask'd if they had yet any
pretence to any Right upon Staten Island, or could pretend to make
any, which was done by ye Secretary Cornelius Van Tienhooven, who
could speak in ye Indian Dialect very well, whereupon they ansered that
they were well satisfied & well agreed with me, & they (ye sd. Indians),
after that made no pretence till ye year 1649—at which time I was in
ye mind to go with my wife, children & people to live upon sd. Island
again. The Indians began then of to speak of buying ye Island again;
I then demonstrated to them ye aforesd. Sale & agreement, which they
acknowledged they knew very well, & that they did not speak of that,
but they supposed that y Island by reason of ye war, by killing, burning
& driving us off, was become theirs again, and therefore that ought
that there must be a new bargain made, which I wholly refused them
& would neither giver, nor promise them any thing saying unto them,*

that which is sold, must remain sold & that ye Dutch will not pay twice for any thing, which they have once bought, but if they will once more have a small gift gratis to maintain good friendship as had been done before I would give it them, whereunto (after mature deliberation among themselves) they resolved; whereupon I gave them amongst them all two Coats of Duffles containing Six Ells four fathom of wampum, 5, or 6, little kittles, some awls & needles wherewith they were all well satisfied & cryed unanimously (Keene, Keene, Keene orit nietap) i.e. Thank you, Thank you, Thank you Good friend, and they were very well satisfied until Lubbert Van Dincklagen began to speak with ye Indians of buying Staten Island again of them, who did it on purpose to find occasion to write to ye Lord Capell to try whether under that Covert he might bring about ye getting of some goods of ye sd. Lord into his hands to dispose thereof for himself & to give little thereof to ye Indians for there is indeed nothing at all due to them for by such means ye Indians would be induced often to make outrages, that they might ev'ry now & then be paid again & not only to play such Prancks upon Staten Island, but throout all New Netherland, where the Lords of ye West India Company's Governmt. Extendeth. I trust therefore that ye honou'd Lords will not approve (or allow) of such bargains, in order to ye preventing more mischiefs.

This is as much as I can write of Testifie of this matter
    This done at Amsterdam ye 30th of Janry 1659—by me—Staten Island is bought for ye use & acct of ye Honble Lords of ye West India Company Augst ye 10. Anno 1630 by their Ministers.

Peter Minnewit	*John Lampo*
Peter Byleveldt	*Reynier Harmenss:*
Jacob Elberts Wissingh	*Symon Derksen Pos.*

    of ye following Indians

Krahorat	*Piearewach*
Tamekap	*Sackwewah*
Tetemackwemama	*Wissipoack*
Wieromies	

As appeared by ye Records of ye date abovesd.

According to the Holland Directors, he "has now arrived here [Netherland] from New England" in 13 February 1659 . . . [75]

> *Cornelis Melyen at ye desire of the Lords of the West India company at their chamber in Amsterdam, declares what be knows concerning ye purchase of Staten Island from the Indians in New Netherland, & what they receiv'd for ye payment of it, Sayith that Anno 1640. (at which time ye aforesd. Lords had granted him License to plant & manure his sd. Colony of Staten Island) he went to ye late Goverar Walter Vantwilder (then being at Amsterdam) of whom he amongst other things Enquired into ye circumstances of ye purchase of Staten Island of ye Indians, who answered him, that ye Island was bought & paid for by ye Governr Minnewit, who immediately preceded him; He desired him (if he could) to do him ye kindness of furnishing him with y relation thereof in writing, wch (at his request) he did, & gave him some days after a written Copy taken out of ye purchac'd deed (or bill of Sale) which shwe'd what pay ye Indians receiv'd for sd, Island, vizt. Some Duffies Kittles, Axes, Hoes, Wampum, Drilling Awls, Jews Harps, and diverse other small wares, which were all particularizd, wch Bill of Sale was signed by diverse Indians & remain in his custody intill ye Dunkirders took him, his Ship, people, Cattle & all his writings—The Year following arriving in New Netherland & being come on Staten Island I (ye sd. Cornelius Melyen) caused ye Indians to be askt whether they were not well recompenced by Minnewit for sd. Island, They gave me for Answer, yt they had sold it to sd. Minnewit & were paid for it, but that it was their custome, when a New Governr came to such a place, that there should be a Gratuity given them; thereby to continue the friendship between ye Indians & or nation, which I did*

All of Melyn's efforts to have his appeal disposed of by the States General were without avail. It remained pending for 11 years and then, he, wearied with delay, broken in fortune by the great losses he had sustained in the Indian Wars of 1643 and 1655 and in his unequal contest with Stuyvesant, surrendered to the Company his rights as Patroon of Staten Island by the following deed . . . [76]

> *Sale & Surrender of Staten Island, by Cornelis Melyn, as Patroon, to the Directors of Amsterdam*

This Day the 14ᵗʰ of June, in the year 1659, acknowledges Mr. Cornelis Melyn, thus far Patroon, and enjoying the Jus Patonatus of the Colonie on Staten Island, situated at the mouth of the North River in New Netherland, for himself, his heirs and posterity, and agreed with the Lords Directors of the Privileged West India Company, and the Department of Amsterdam, voluntarily, in the following manner: He shall and will make a cession and transfer of all his authority, pre-eminence, jurisdictions, prerogatives, advantages, emuluments, privileges and exemptions, which he as Patroon enjoyed, in the lands and over the inhabitants of the Colonie of Staten Island, with all its consequences, appendices and dependencies, without any exception, which he obtained, as well by resolutions, acts and articles of privileges and exemptions, as by open letters, which Were granted him by the Director Willem Kieft, deceased, in New Netherland; and by other letters confirming his claims, which might yet have been produced, without exception, all which he shall deliver to the aforesaid Department both here and in New Netherland, as far as these can be discovered.

Provided, that by the aforesaid Company and Department, shall in New Netherland to him be reimbursed all such money as have been obtained from the sale of a dwelling house, situated on the Manhattans in New Amsterdam, near the Fort, which was sold by the Director-general Stuyvesant, by execution I behalf of Daniel Michaelson, skipper of the ship, The New Netherland Fortune, in so far this money is yet in the possession of the Company; and besides that shall be paid to him here in ready cash, the sum of fifteen hundred guilders; and further that he shall enjoy the freedom and exemptions, as well here as in New Netherland, from recognitions, to the amount of about one thousand guilders in wares and merchandise, necessary articles for husbandry, or similar permitted goods, which he might conclude to transport with him to New Netherland; and further, that he with his family and attendants shall be transported thither either in a hired vessel, or in one belonging to the Company, at the Company's expense, in conformity to present usage. Further, that he, too, shall as a free Colonist and Inhabitant, possess for himself and his posterity, as free and allodial property, all the lands, houses and lots which he thus far possessed, or might in future possess (and of which no other person had taken possession), or to the inheritance of which he may be entitled either by a last will, codicil, donation or legacy, or by contract or I any other manner, to dispose of these, agreeably to the articles of freedom and exemptions which were granted to the Patroons and Colonists; that whenever his oldest son shall be of age, and be competent to execute the office, and a Sheriff in aforesaid Colonie, shall be wanted he shall be preferred, by the Company and Department of Amsterdam, above all others; and finally that the Company shall procure him by whether these regard the Company, or their Province, or whatever subject these may relate to, which existed before, and shall now be entirely obliterated, so that henceforewrd they shall treat one another as good friends and with respect, and assist one another whenever it shall be in their power.

For all which the aforesaid Cornelis Melyn submits his person and property, real and personal, present and future, without any exception, to the control of the Court of Justice in Holland, and to that of all other Courts and judges, as well in New Netherland as here. In good faith and truth whereof, have subscribed the Directors and Commissaries, appointed and authorized by their Brethren for this special purpose, on the 10th of April last, and signed by the aforesaid Cornelis Melyn, in Amsterdam on the day and year mentioned above. Was signed Edwrd Man, as Director; Abraham Wilmer-Donck, as Director; H. Bontemartel, as Director; Cornelis Melyn, former Patroon of Staten Island.

By this instrument, it will be noticed; Melyn did not surrender but retained his land on Staten Island.

Before 1655, the Company had decided not to establish any more Patroonships, and possibly they considered this a good opportunity to get rid of Melyn as on 13 June 1659, they entered into an agreement with him for the purchase of his right of Patroonship of Staten Island. The agreement also involved the payment to Melyn for his confiscated real estate and some of other matters . . . [77]

Upon this thirteenth Day of June 1659—Mr. Cornelius Melyen (who until this time hath been Patron, & hath had Jus Patronatus of ye Colony and Staten Island scituated in ye mouth of ye North River in New Netherland) for himself, his heirs & Successors acknowledgeth to have bargained & agreed wth the Lords ye Directors of ye privileged West India Company at their chamber here in Amsterdam freely &

most amicably by these presents (Vizt) That he consenteth to desist deliver over, transfer & Transport all ye Pow'r, Authority, Highness, Jurisdiction, preheminencies, prerogatives, Profitts, Emoluments, Liberties, & exemptions belonging to him in quality of Patroon & belonged to him until now in upon ye lands & Colony of ye sd. Staten Island with ye following dependencies & appendencies thereof none excepted by him procured, according to ye Resolutions, Acts, articles, freedoms & exemptions & other instruments as likewise by ye letters of conveyance made over especially unto him by Willm. Kieft Governor of New Netherland, & other letters of concessions, which may have been granted concerning ye same, non excepted, which he also agreeth to deliver up unton ye abovementioned Chamber, as well here as in New Netherland as many as are yet in his custody & possession are made to cease Expressly upon ye following conditions Vizt. That ye abovementioned company & chamber shall in New Netherland make restitution of all such Sum or Sums of money, which were produced from certain his houseings & Lotts scituated & being upon ye Manhatans in New Amsterdam neer ye ffort (which were sold by Governor Stuyvesandt by Execution in behalf of Daniel Michiels master of ye Ship ye New Netherland's Fortune) Shall be restored to him again in New Netherland by sd. Company & chamber for ye sd. Moneys or so much thereof as yet may be found to remain with ye sd. Company.

And moreover that ye Just Sume of fifteen hundred gilders shall be forthwith paid him, & likewise that he shall enjoy ye Freedome & exemption of ye Custome both here & in New Netherland of ye value of about one thousand gilders Stock of Merchandise, being necessary utensels for cultivating land & permitted, wch he should think fitt to carry wth him into New Netherland.

As likewise that himself, his family & his people wth him shall be transported over thither with their own ships or ships hired at ye charge of the company according to ye Prsent use. Also that he for ye future as a free Coloneer & inhabitant for himself & his Successors shall hold & possess as free & legal estate, ye lands houses & lotts, which he hath there in ye sd. Colony & hath hitherto made use of & which he yet shall be able to improve (& by others not possessed) they shall enjoy ye Succession thereof or by will, writings, donation or gift, agreemt. Or otherwise may dispose thereof, as according to ye Articles of Privilege & Exemptions granted to Patroons & Coloneers. That likewise his eldest son being capable (& ye sd. Colony having need of a Schout, & one to be appointed thereupon) shall be preferred before any other by ye aforesd. Company & Chamber. And Finally that by ye present Governor Steuyvesandt shall be shewed & maintained a perfect Amnestia of all strifes, hatred & differences, which formerly may have risen between them; as well in respect of ye Company as their own private concerns; ye same hereby to remain forgiven & for ye future they to be good friends & to respect & acknowledge each other in his quality & to demonstrate all reasonable assistance. To ye performance all ye premises He Cornelius Melyen bindeth himself & his estate movable and unmovable, present & future none excepted to ye Submission of ye Court of Holland & all laws & Judges as well in New Netherland as herein this Countrey—In Witness whereof this is underwritten by ye undernamed Lords & Committee of ye West India Company thereunto authoriz'd by ye Lords their fellow brethren on ye behalf of ye aforementioned company & chamber by special Comission dated ye tenth of April last past, & by ye sforesd. Cornelius Melyen at Amsterdam ye day & year aforesd. Was underwritten & signed. Edward Man as Direct. Abraham Wilmerdonck as Directr H: Bontemantel as Directr Cornelius Melyen late Patroon of Staten Island in ye presence of me as Notary, H: Schaelf No. P.

It agreeth with ye original signed agreement being in my Custody In Witness H: Shaef Noy Public

Examined this with ye Dutch agreemt. & find it to be a true translate to ye best of my understanding as Witness my hand Jacob Leisler Also by me vera copia George Turfry

Endorsed: A Copy of ye Translate of ye Agreement of Melyen wth ye West India Company Examd Pr Mr. Leisler.

Melyn arrived with an understanding with the West India Company where he resigned his claim to the Island. He received 1500 guilders, an indemnity for his losses, the promise of certain privileges as a "free colonist and inhabitant" in New Netherland and a "full amnesty with regard to all disputes" . . . [78]

Voyage 12: 1659, Holland to New Netherland

Melyn, his two sons and two others, Jacob and Isaac, departed Holland after 14 October 1659 on the ship, *De Liefde* (*The Love*) and arrived in New Netherlands on 5 March 1660 to their new home in New Haven, Connecticut. Cornelis was in and out of court in New Haven continually until his death as apparently his background didn't mix well with the Puritan way of life. Janneken's name appears in records until 1674.

More court transactions involving Cornelius . . . [79-84]

> *(8 June 1660), Cornelis Melein, pltf. v/s Sybout Claze, deft. Pltf. concludes in writing, that deft. Shall be condemned to pay him the sum of fl. 550. In beavers with interest thereof for purchase of a lot bought in the beginning of April 1651. Which lost is built on. On condition of deducting what is paid thereon proving the same. Deft. Demands copy. The Court order copy to be furnished to party, to answer thereunto at the next Court day.*

> *(15 June 1660). Order, on the answer of Sybout Clazen in convention and demand I reconvention against Cornelis Melyn:-The Court order copy to be furnished to party thereunto to answer at the next Court day.*

> *(22 June 1660). On the reply in convention and answer in reconvention of Cornelis Melein, ordered:-The Court order copy to be furnished to party to answer thereunto at the next Court day.*

> *(31 August 1660), The Burgomaster and Schepens of the City Amsterdam in New Netherland have considered, read and re-read the pieces, documents and papers used on both sides in the suit between Cornelis Meleyn, pltf., at and against Sybout Claze, deft. The pltf. demands payment from the deft. For certain lot which he sold the deft. for the sum of five hundred and fifty guilders in beavers with interest thereon; to which the deft. always answers, he is ready to pay for the purchased lot, refusing solutum, and says that the pltf. has failed to give him proper conveyance thereof; requests therefore that the reckoning with each other may be in the presence of arbitrators, proposing before the removing the conveyance to assign what then*

shall be found belonging to him; and demanding in reconvention, inasmuch as he could sell the said lot twice and it not being conveyed, he was prevented, not being able to deliver it, that the pltf. shall be condemned to make good the loss and interest, incurred thereby, such being found onsistent with justice. Burgomaster and Schepens having considered and weighed all that is material, find that parties have not come to any final settlement with each other, therefore refer the matter to the Honorable Oloff Stevensen Cortland, old Burgomaster and now Treasurer of this City, and the Honorable Paulus Leendersten van der Grift, also Old Burgomaster and late Treasurer of this City, to examine and settle parties a/cs on both sides, and if possible to reconcile them; if not to report their proceedings to the Court. Done as above.

(5 October 1660), Ritchert Smith, pltf. v/s Cornlis Melein, deft. PLtf. demands of deft. payment of a note for the sum of f. 114. Signed by deft's wife, the same to be paid in beaver; relating at length the circumstances, from which it arose. Deft. says, that for the payment of nine pounds sterling which he owned Mr. Smitt, he agreed with him for two ankers of strong water, which he should come and draw from Staten Island, keeping them for Mr. Smitt, and that Mr. Smitt promised to do so, either himself or by another. And the ankers lay a long time before they were taken away. Meanwhile the war broke out with the Indians, who destroyed everything, taking himself and his people prisoners. Maintains he is not bound to make the same good, saying further, that Mr. Smitt accompanied by some Englishmen came to his wife whilst he was in Holland and forced her to sign the note. Pltf. denies it all. The Court order Cornelis Meleyn to prove, that he agreed about the payment of the nine pounds sterling by the two ankers of strong waters, and when Mr. Smitt should draw the two ankers of strong water from Staten Island, and further that his wife was constrained to sign the note exhibited by Mr. Smitt.

(15 February 1661), Cornelis Melein appears in Court exhibiting the decision of arbitrators, dated 10: 7ber 1660, appointed by the Court a given in the case between him and Sybout Clasen and approved by them: Requests therefore fulfillment thereof. Burgomasters and Schepens having seen and read the decision approved and laud the same, and order Sybout Clasen to fulfill and pay to Cornelis Meleyn.

They started at once to obtain from Stuyvesant the confiscated property, but with no success . . . [85]

> *In the year after the birth of our Lord and Savior Jesus Christ one thousand six hundred for and forty the 17ʰ day of December, appeared before me Cornelis Van Tienhoven, Secretary of New Netherland, Burger Jorisen, Farrier (hoefsmid) and inhabitant here, who declared in the presence of the below subscribed witnesses to convey and transfer in a tru free ownership to Mr. Cornelis Melyn, his house and lot situated on the island Manhatans, as he is by these presents conveying and transferring said lot and house by virtue of ground brief & conveyance granted by the Director and Councillors of New Netherland, dated April 28, 1643. On account whereof he Burger Jorisen Constitutes in his stead as real and actual owner of the said lot and house said Cornelis Melyn or those entering upon his right, granting him irrevocable power, authority and what has been expressed before, so that he, Melyn, may do with and dispose of the same as he might do with other his patrimonial estate, without he, the grantor, retaining in the same any ownership or claim (the bill of sale having been satisfied), but renouncing the same from now on for ever. In testimony herof, the Minute of the present has been subscribed to at the record office by Burger Jorissen, Will. De Kay & Gysbert Opdyck, as witnesses invited for this purpose. Done at For Amsterdam in New Netherland, December 17, 1644, New Style.*
>
> *In was subscribed to with the mark Burger Jorisen and signed in the name of Burger Jorisen.*
>
> *On March 18 1661 the here standing name has been put down by Burger Jorisse.*
>
> *To which we testify*
>
> *N. de Sille, N. Bayard*
>
> *A true copy taken from the Records being much toorne (signed) David Jamison.*
>
> *D: Secry.*
>
> *Endorsed in Dutch: Conveyance of Burger Joris to Cornelis Melyn, December 17ʰ, 1644.*

The articles of the agreement seemed to have constantly been under discussion between Stuyvesant and Melyn as Melyn was summoned before the Council on 23 May 1661 to settle all the articles of dispute. The principle disagreement was the sale of the Island. Melyn's intent was to agree to relinquish his rights of the Patroonship, but that to retain his right to the soil, i.e., the title to the land itself. Stuyvesant stuck by the true meaning of the agreement, limited Melyn to the land for cultivation. He could use the land for himself but not sell to others . . . [86]

> *Invited to be present at the meeting, and standing inside, Cornelis Melyn; after taking up the Contract entered into by the Hon. Heeren Managers and the said Melyn in date of June 13, 1659, in regard to Staten Island, said Melyn was asked whether he had in his possession any papers and documents regarding said Island, and whether he was prepared in conformity with said contract, to deliver the same to the Director General and Councillors, and further to convey said Island in behalf of the privileged West India Company at the Chamber of Amsterdam, excepting the lands, houses and lots he is occupying or may be able to occupy as per the said contract.*

> *Whereto it was answered in substance by the said Cornelis Melyn that he was ready to hand to the Director General & Council the papers and documents concerning the same, in his possession, which he has also immediately done, delivering the papers specified below, declaring to have no others concerning the said island; in regard to the transfer and conveyance of the said island in behalf of the Hon. Priv. West India Company (excepting the lands, houses and lots he is occupying there etc.) said this had never been his opinion, but only that he should grant, convey, cede and transfer all the power, authority, rights, jurisdiction, preeminence, prerogatives, etc. belonging to him in his quality as patroon of the said island; requested on the contrary since he had now surrendered the deed granted to him for said island by the deceased Heer Kieft, that he should again be granted a new deed for the ownership of the said island.*

> *It was answered if it had been the intention that he should remain possessed of the said entire island why it should have been necessary to stipulate that for himself and his heirs he shall hold and retain as a free allodial possession that lands, houses and lots owned and up to now occupied by him, and which he may yet be able to acquire etc.; and further if the entire island belongs to him, what, then, the Heeren Mangers have bought of the heirs of the Lord Van Capelle, who have now also conveyed their right to the Hon. Company?*

In regard to which said Cornelius Melyn acknowledged having ceded and vacated one third of the said island to the Lord Capelle, but that he even yet had large claims against the same; in regard to the two remaining thirds, it had not been his opinion-as expressed before-to renounce his ownership; but that it would be well to enquire how the Hon. Heeren managers understand the same.

Said Melyn was also informed that he had been charged for his own passage and for that of he servants taken with him, just like others, carried over at the expense of the Company, because it is stipulated in the said Contract that he shall be conveyed with his family at the expense of the Company that he shall be conveyed with his family at the expense of the Company, as is at present customary: which means that the advanced passage money be here refunded. Said Melyn maintains, that it is his opinion and was also the opinion of the Hon. Heeren managers that he was his people were to be carried over absolutely free of charge, without repaying the advanced moneys; also because he was granted freedom of tolls on a thousand guilders principal, and not having taken with him so large a principal (capital) from Holland he would be permitted to deduct the balance here I paying duties or tolls.

After divers debated for and against it was resolved to send a copy of the present to the Hon. Heeren Mangers and not to proceed with this business, until we shall have received further explanation regarding said contract of said Heeren Managers.

Acted on the date written above.

The papers surrendered by Mr. Cornelis Melyn concerning Staten Island are as follows:

A petition of Cornelis Melyn to the Hon. Heeren Managers, and disposition on the same, by which he is permitted to found a colony on Staten Island and he is acknowledged as Patroon, dated July 3, 1640.

A further petition of said Melyn to the Heeren Managers dated Feb. 18, 1641, presented after he had been taken by the Duynkerckers, requesting leave to depart with wife, children, servants and some cattle in Company's ships for New Netherland.

Two extracts of resolution of the Hon. Heeren Managers dated 18ᵗʰ and 25ᵗʰ February, 1641, by which the afore said consent is renewed.

A groundbrief being the conveyance of the Staten Island to Cornelis Melyn granted in consequence of the consent mentioned above, signed by the Heer General William Kieft, dated June 19, 1642.

Agrees with the aforesaid Register,
C.V. Ruyven, Secretary.
Govr Steuyvesant in Council, his Evil construction of ye agreemt of ye West India Company & Melyen.

This is an extract from a letter for the Hon. Heeren, Managers to the Messrs. Director and Councillors of New Netherland of 27 January 1662 . . . [87]

Concerning the contention of Cornelis Melyn that he surely did sell and deliver to the company the title and the right of patroonship of the Staten Island, but not the lands themselves, we can not observe that the same can be deduced from the contract entered into with him concerning the same, but assured by the opposite, as there is entered, as your Honors have justly remarked and argued against him, that from now on, as free colonist and inhabitant, he shall have and hold for himself and his descendants as a free, allodial possession the lands, houses and losts he had in said colony and has occupied hitherto and which he shal yet be able to occupy. Ergo not the remaining lands which are laying gallow and uncultivated, so that the same neither can or must be permitted to be questioned.

Agrees with the Letter mentioned above, C.V. Ruyven.

Court transactions involving Janneken . . . [88-90]

(7 Mar 1662), Jannetje Melyns, pltf. v/s Arien Symonzen, deft. Deft. in default.

(14 Mar 1662), Jannetje Melyns, pltf. v/s Arien Symonzen, deft. Both in default.

(8 Oct 1662), "Mr. Moline and his wife" were in Court to plead for mitigation of a sentence upon their son Jacob. The testimony of Cornelis

Melyn and his wife "was interpreted by Mr. Goodenhouse" indicating
that their command of English was not sufficient to warrant them
testifying in that language.

By 1665, Cornelius was registered to pay taxes as he is listed on the tax
roll in New Amsterdam. Between 1665 and 1674, he died in New Haven,
Connecticut. On a list of the Burghers and Inhabitants of this city, he is listed
as a resident of The Heere Graft, in New Amsterdam. The marriage of two
of Melyn's daughters in New Haven on 25 August 1664 may well mark the
breaking up of the Melyn home . . . [91]

Appeared before me William Bogardus Notary Publick in New-York,
admitted by ye Honble Francis Lovelace by his Royal highness James
Duke of York & Albany etc. Governr General of all his Territories
in America & before ye afternamed Witnesses; Yochem Beekman,
aged about 49 years, & Thomas Koninck aged about 55 years both
inhabitants of this City at ye request of Mr. Jacob Melyen, who verbally
inste'd of a Solemn Oath attest & declare, that now about 30 years
since according to their best remembrance being in service of ye West
India Company as Souldiers, were present upon Staten Island when ye
former Sachems & owners of Staten Island aforesd. Had some difference
with sd. Melyens Father Cornelius Melyen about ye free hunting. Upon
ye aforesd. Island, which ye sd. Cornelius Melyen, conceives that they
parted with their right of at their Sale, & after some debates more ye
sd Jacob Melyen's Father referred it to Nichos kartenz Noorman, who
was interpreter, when ye Sale of ye aforemention'd Isld. Was made, &
would make it appear by him, wherewith ye Indians were satisfied,
whereupon ye aforesd. Nicho: Kartenz by sd. Jacob Melyen's Father
was sent for the come to sd. Staten island, & ye aforesd. Sachems
& owners were thereupon assembled together, again, whereupon ye
aforesd. Niche:s Kartenz (by sd. Jacob Melyen's Father's desire) related
unto them what pay they had received for that & for ye afresd. Island,
Vizt. Some Duffles, Blanckets, Axes, Kittles, Wampum—Wherewith
ye Indians were convinced, who then declared that they could not well
be without the Liberty of Hunting & desired Earnestly to agree with
ye sd. Melyens Father, what they shall yearly contribute to him for its
whereupon then was agreed that they should yearly contribute to him
for it; whereupon then was agreed that they should yearly contribute &
deliver Ten or Twelve Deer & some Turkeys not remembering the Just

Quantity, & ye Deponts further declare that they were present & did so that some Deer for ye fulfilling ye promised contribution were deliver'd to ye aforesd. Melyen's Father; concluding herewith their Deposition & are ready in case of need & desired to confirm it by Oath. This done at New York upon Manhatans Island in presence of Henry Williams, Baker, & Adolph Pieters Carpenter as witnesses hereunto desired who have signed unto these presents with me Notary Pubck underwritten June 27, Anno 1672 (???)
Agreth with ye Original, wch
Testifieth
W Bogardus Botay Pubck

Endorsed: Several Testimonies & writings relating to ye Purchase of Staten Island

The New Haven land records has an undated deed which "Johannah Melyn, widow of New Haven" sold the property which Cornelis Melyn had purchased from Lieutenant Seely to Henry Glover, from which it may be inferred that Melyn by an unrecorded will, gave the property to his wife. "Samuel van Goodenhousen and Jacob Melein" witnessed this deed, which was recorded on 31 July 1685 . . . [92]

Furthermore it is agreed upon that Mr. Goodenhouse shall possess the house till his yeare be up only Goodman Glover is to have the chamber where I lye.

On 27 July 1685, Henry Glover placed on record a declaration that several described pieces of property (one being the Melyn home property) had formerly belonged to him. And that by deed of gift, he had passed them to his son John Glover at or about the time of his marriage to Johanna Glover, which was on 7 December 1671 in New Haven. The sale of the Melyn home probably marked the final departure of Janneken Melyn from New Haven. Some of their children were living in New Haven as late as 1668. There is little known of Janneken other than her witnessing a baptism of one of her grandchildren, Samuel Winans, on 2 April 1672.

In a petition to Governor Colve, dated "New Orange, 1674, Apr 12/2," Jacob Melyn mentions "my aged mother" which is the last reference of her as being alive that has been found. A "Request of the Children of Heirs of the late Cornelis Melyn" in regard to the Staten Island property of 5 October

of 1674, was prepared and sent to the authorities at Albany. This petition
is signed by the five surviving children in the order of their ages. Janneken
is not mentioned as being alive or deceased. According to the minute book
of the New York Mayor's Court, 23 March 1674 or 1675, in the case of
George Davis, Plaintiff vs. Administrators of Anna Molyne, Defendant,
reads: "The Plaintiff declared for 345 Carolus guilders due to his wife from
the said Anna Molyne. The Court orders that the attachments continue on
the house and a copy of the declaration be ready for the defendants." On
28 May 1684, after Janneken's death, the second house lot was conveyed by
their son, Jacob . . . [93]

> *It is curious fact that this small plat of ground has retained its
> dimensions though the vicissitudes of nearly two centuries and a half,
> and is today occupied by a small and somewhat dingy brick building
> with a wealth of rusty fire-escapes; it appears to have resisted absorption
> by the more imposing structure whose blank wall of yellow brick
> overtower it on two sides.*

The New York Historical Society has a large number of papers relating
to Cornelis Melyn which was donated by J.D. Sergeant of Philadelphia,
Pennsylvania, a Melyn descendant. Among them is the original Writ of
clause from Stuyvesant's sentence dated 28 April 1648, the stay the appeal
was allowed, and letters and petitions for Cornelis Melyn and his son Jacob
in reference to Staten Island. [94]

In 1913, Dodd and Livingston, booksellers in New York, had for sale at
the price of $2,500.00 five manuscripts relating to Staten Island and Cornelis
Melyn: (1.) The safe conduct of States General to Melyn and Kuyter dated
1 May 1648; (2.) A second warrant for the safe conduct and protection of
Melyn, dated 30 June 1650. This was issued after Stuyvesant had refused
to obey the first and Melyn had returned to Holland and was about to sale
for New Amsterdam in the ship *New Netherlands Fortune* fitted out at the
expense of Baron Von Der Capellen and other merchants with the purpose
of colonizing Staten Island; (3.) Contract between Melyn and Lord Hendrick
Von Der Capellen for a part of Staten Island, dated 4 June 1650; (4.) A letter
of Melyn dated 25 June 1652, mentioned above; and (5.) Agreement between
Cornelis Melyn and the West India Company, by which he relinquished his
patroonship of Staten Island, dated Amsterdam, 13 June 1659.

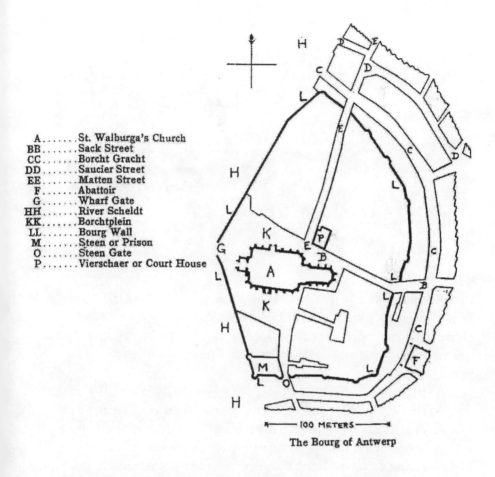

A......St. Walburga's Church
BB......Sack Street
CC......Borcht Gracht
DD......Saucier Street
EE......Matten Street
F......Abattoir
G......Wharf Gate
HH......River Scheldt
KK......Borchtplein
LL......Bourg Wall
M......Steen or Prison
O......Steen Gate
P......Vierschaer or Court House

The Bourg of Antwerp

A drawing of a portion of the Bourg of Antwerp, Belgium and
some of the adjacent streets, based on the plan facing page 96,
Vol. 1 of Mertens and Torgs: "Geschiedenis van Antwerpen."

(Paul Gibson Burton, "The Antwerp Ancestry of Cornelius Melyn,"
The New York Genealogical and Biographical Record, Vol. 67, page 255.)

Betrothal Certificate of Cornelis Melyn and Janneken Adriaens

Cornelius Melyn

Appeared *as before Cornelius Melyn from Antwerp, aged 35 years, having no parents, leather dresser, living in the Elant Street, assigned by Geraert Lodewijsz [and] Jannetie Arienss from Myert, aged 23 years, having no parents, living on the LIndegracht, assisted by Engel Thomas.*

Requesting their three Sunday banns, in order to solemnize thereafter the aforesaid marriage, and to consummate it, provided however no lawful impediment thereto be disclosed. And inasmuch as they declared in truth that they were free persons, and were not related to each other in blood in such a way as to prevent a Christian marriage, their banns have been allowed to them.

Bethrothal Certificate of Cornelius Melyn and Janneken Adriaens. The italics indicate the words which correspond to the Dutch words that are written into the original certificate.

(Paul Gibson Burton, "The Antwerp Ancestry of Cornelius Melyn," *The New York Genealogical and Biographical Record*, Vol. 68, page 3.)

New Amsterdam on Manhattan, looking west.
Cornelius Melyn's home in Section "O".

(*http://www.teachout.org/vna/map.html.*)

Arrow indicating location of Cornelius Melyn's home by the Graft in New Amsterdam by 1655.

(J. H. Innes, *New Amsterdam and Its People*, 1902)

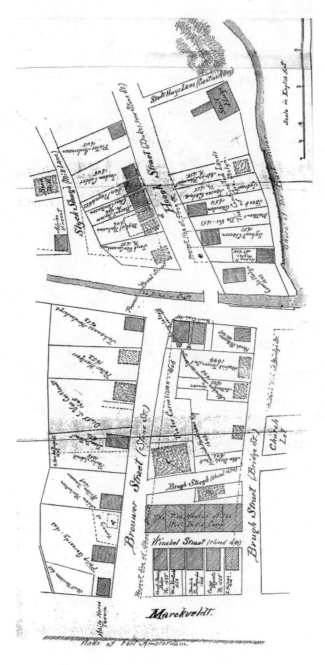

The East River Shore near the "Graft," 1652

AA. Houses on the Marckveldt
BB. Houses on the Marckveldt Steegh and Never Graft
CC. Rear of the "Five Houses"
D.   Brewery of the West India Co.
E.   Old Church
F.   Old Parsonage (Hendr. Jansen Smit)
G.   Hendricksen Kip
H.   Anthony Jansen van Vees
I.   Hendr. Jansen Smit
J.   Hendr. Willemsen, backer
K.   Houses of Tennis Craie
L.   Jacob Wolphertsen van Couwenhoven
M.   Cornelius Melyn
N.   Capt. Tochem PIetersen Kuyter
O.   Sibout Claessen
P.   Cornelis van Tienhoven (aft. Jacob Steendam)
Q.   Adriaen Vincent.

(J.H. Innes, *New Amsterdam and Its People*, 1902, p. 104)

Cornelius' Children and Some Descendants

Cornelia Melyn

Cornelius and Jannetken Melyn's first child, Cornelia, was born and baptized on the same day, 27 February 1628, in Nieuwe Kerk, Amsterdam, which was witnessed by Heyltje de Raet. She immigrated with her parents on the ship, *Den Eyckenboom* (*The Oak Tree*) that sailed from Holland on 17 May 1641 and arrived in New Amsterdam, New York shortly before 15 August 1641. [95]

[She] was, in her day, the belle of New Amsterdam, and was sought for by the principal aspirants to the felicities of matrimony. Her father, unlike most of those who immigrated to this colony in early times, was a man of considerable wealth on his arrival her in 1639. After examining into the prospects and resources and conditions of the country, he returned to the fatherland, where he procured a patient for a large portion of State Island, and having decided upon establishing his residence here, he brought his family in the year 1641 and at once commenced colonizing the extensive territory of which he was patron. He also had a residence in New Amsterdam on the present Northeast corner of Pearl and Bread streets, then a pleasant place of residence facing the East River. Here the youthful Cornelia grew to the estate of womanhood, the admired and envied of the neighbors. None of the youth of the community were of sufficient condition to make pretension to the aristocratic beauty, until Captain Loper, the Commander of the Dutch ship of war permanently stationed in the harbor, put forth his claims, which met with a favorable response. The marriage took place with great festivities in the year 1647. The married life of this distinguished couple did not prove of long duration, for the Captain died within three or four years, and his widow, in the year 1655,

married Jacob Schellinger, a merchant of high standing, resident of
New Amsterdam.

Like her mother, Cornelia's life was long and eventful; her memories must have embraced Antwerp, Belgium in its decaying splendor, and New Amsterdam, New York with no splendor at all, merely a few thatched cottages around the fort. She remembered Staten Island as an unbroken wilderness, and her father's plantation there, twice destroyed by Indians, and the days of panic and distress in the little house on the Graft in New Amsterdam. Then came the long struggles of her father against the colonial maladministration and his self-imposed exile from New Amsterdam during the many years of which the care of his family had devolved largely upon herself. She had seen the village of huts at New Amsterdam grow into a town of importance and had seen the English rule supplant that of the Dutch. Of her father's two great enemies so well known to her, she could remember how the life of one had closed in horror in the wreck of the *Princess* (which her brother and her pastor also perished) and how the other had ended his days in seclusion and in bitter humiliation at his farmhouse up the Bouwery Land on Manhattan Island. A trivial incident from the Council Minutes of New Netherland perhaps can help in showing something of Cornelia's character. Gerrit Hendricksen, aged 11-12 years, made a deposition on 23 November 1644 that while Jacob Melyn, aged 4 years, was standing with his dog by a wall, holding a piece of bread in his hand. Gerrit threw a piece of broken pottery at the dog, but it hit Jacob in the eye. Cornelia, aged 16 years, flew at Gerrit and struck him. Her kerchief fell from her shoulders and Gerrit stepped on it and it was torn. This disposition was made at Cornelius' request.

On 30 June 1647, Cornelia and Captain Jacobus Lugt de Loper, had their banns published in the New York Dutch Church of New Amsterdam. He was a Swede from Stockholm . . . [96]

. . . who came out in the ship Swol in the year 1643 as Commander
and Captain Lieutenant."

Cornelia and Jacobus had only two children, James and Joanna. There are a number of resolutions, from 1643 to 1644, signed by Jacob de Loper and from other entries it would seem that he was a Commandant at Curacao in 1646. On 14 June 1649, he presented a petition to the Council at New Netherland requesting permission to take his sloop to the South (Delaware) River, but was denied ostensibly because he had married Cornelia Melyn, who at that time was in the midst of his struggle with Stuyvesant. The Council Minute states that the denial was in accordance with the instructions of the Directors of the West Indian Company (27 January 1649). The reference was apparently to the following sentence in the letter of that date from the Directors to Stuyvesant . . . [97]

> . . . *Cornelius Melyn, who has always had a bad reputation and who, as we understand, will do everything to create trouble and mischief for us on the side towards the Swedish colony* . . .

. . . i.e., the Delaware. On 14 August 1649, Loper, who describes himself, " . . . as at present a burgher here . . ." gave a Power of Attorney to his father-in-law, Cornelius Melyn, then departing to Holland, to collect for him 2311 guilders, 5 stuivers and 12 pennies, less 660 guilders and 15 stuivers, the balance due him for services in Curacao. Loper died between 4 January 1651 (a signed note) and 7 April 1653 (banns of marriage of his widow to Jacob Schellinger which were published in the New York Dutch Church).

On 7 April 1653, Cornelia entered into banns of marriage with Jacobus Schellinger in the Old Dutch Church, New York. They lived on Staten Island with or near her father. After their marriage, they lived some 12 to 13 years in New Amsterdam. Jacob was captured by Indians during the Staten Island massacre of September 1655. His home was burned and laid waste by the Indians. This burning resulted in several suits by Amsterdam merchants whom he represented, demanding an accounting for cargoes sent by them to be sold on commission. Jacob's defense was that the goods were not salable wares, and that after sending them to various places, he at last took them to his house on Staten Island, where they, with his own property, were burned by Indians. While some of these goods had been sold, it was impossible for him to determine the amount, since his account books had also been destroyed. He was ordered by the Court to prove what goods were sold, and what was destroyed. He was apparently unable to do so as on 12 August 1658, he was imprisoned but soon escaped. On 27 August 1658, the Court ordered that some of his goods, which had been distained, should be sold to defray the costs of his arrest and imprisonment. He escaped confinement; he probably fled to New Haven, Connecticut where Cornelius was living. Soon after, he probably went to New London, where on 24 October 1661, "a Dutchman and his wife" requested a grant of land. On 26 October 1663 at New London "Mr. Skillinger propounded the sale of his house and land this day-None offered anything." A Mrs. Houghton summoned "Mrs. Skillinger" before the

Commissioners on 30 June 1664 to answer for abusing her daughter in the meeting house. The Court instructed Mrs. Houghton "to tutor her daughter better and not occasion disturbances in the meeting house, by any unmeet carriage to her betters hereafter." In 1666, Jacob was possibly still in New London as he was assessed there, but by 2 October 1667 he is described in a deed as of East Hampton, Long Island.

Easthampton, Long Island, New York

On their journey to Easthampton, emerged from the 2 or 3 miles of woodland road which lay between their new home and the sloop that brought them to the "Three-Mile Harbor," the port of Easthampton in Gardiner's Bay, they could see before them the fields of the new settlement, stretching in long strips. Sixteen or 17 years of cultivation had checkered the plain with alternating patches of wheat and rye, of maize and tobacco, and near the houses here and there a young orchard was growing up, or upon spots of greensward, the flax lay rotting in long brownish rows. Along the capacious village street, lined by a couple of score of low thatched cottages (some probably still of their original log construction), no rows of great elms stretched as at present, but the grass grew thickly in its broad space where perhaps the cattle, just returned fro the Common Pasture, gather at their owners' bars and gates, or at the farther end of the street crowded to drink at the Town Pond. Upon the grassy bank (designed for a burial-ground) beyond the pond stood the little thatched church, and still farther in the distance, beyond the green slopes of the "Calf Pasture," the white sand dunes shut out the ocean.

Jacobus was one of the most well-to-do men of the community, and is early assessed at the second highest figure in town. His stepson, Jacobus or James Loper, then a young man just grown up, he would soon acquire the grant of a new parcel of land a short distance east of his stepfather's home, on the north side of the road to the Three-Mile Harbor. Jacobus purchased in October 1667, from Benjamin Conkling, his home lot of 20 acres on the north side of the main street of Easthampton.

About 1668-1669, Jacobus and his stepson turned to whale fishing, then profitable at the eastern end of Long Island, for a number of years at Southampton. They employed the neighboring Montauk Indians as their whaling crews, who were experts in the craft; and their is an agreement still extant by Schellinger and Loper with 13 of the Indians, of 4 July 1675, in which the former agreed to furnish the necessary boats, and to cart the products of the fishery a distance not exceeding two miles for the purpose of trying or boiling; the Indians to receive one half of the profits. He resided in East Hampton where he was involved in numerous real estate transactions. The Schellingers indeed appear to have been somewhat prone to dealings with the Indians, and a curious indenture of apprenticeship still exists, important as showing at what an early date domestic relations were established between the Easthampton settlers and the Montauk Indians. In this document a certain "Muntauket Indian commonly name Papasequiin" and his wife agree with Jacobus Schellinger and his son Jacob to bind out to the latter "our sonn named Quausuch, ould now above seaven yeares the time of apprenticeship was to run from "rimo Aprill at ye yeare eightie eight" and was to extend to 1 April 1698, at which time, besides certain payments to the father, incase of good behavior, etc, of the lad, the latter was to receive the sum of ten pounds in money or goods. Jacobus died on 25 February 1716 or 1717 and Cornelia on 25 February 1717, both in East Hampton. Both supposed to be buried in the churchyard in Easthampton.

Cornelia and Jacobus Loper:

i.   James
ii.   Joanna

Cornelia and Jacobus Schellinger:

iii. William
iv.   Catharine/Catalyntje
v.   Jacobus
vi.   Abraham
vii. Daniel Loper
viii. Cornelius

GENERATION I

Jacobus Loper and Cornelia Melyn

JAMES LOPER, b./bapt. 25 October 1648 Dutch Church, Hendrik Kip and Janneken Molyns were witnesses; orphaned at an early age; became apprentice to Hans Alvers (or Albers) of Milford, Connecticut; 1660, burnt down house next door to his master's hoping that the blaze would reach his master's house, and when it did not, he set fire to Alvers' house also, and was caught in the act before much damage had resulted; apparently tried to "lie out of it," but finally confessed, stating that he had done so to be sent home to his mother. On 11 December 1660, he was sentenced to be whipped, and to pay double for the damage he caused, L100, in addition to the value of the house. If he couldn't afford this or if others wouldn't pay for him, he would be sold as a servant. On 27 May 1661, Richard Baldwin attached some bedding that then belonged to Hans Alvers, and which it was claimed to belong to James Loper, who was still in prison, and had no representation. Baldwin asked that James be sold as a servant to Barbados and the proceeds of the sale was to satisfy the Baldwin's claim. The court decided against this and to have James Whipped instead and then be delivered to Alvers, who was to put him out of

the jurisdiction. James' goods were to remain under custody until the charges of his imprisonment were to be satisfied. On 26 May 1662, the court ordered James' goods be sold and the Marshal of Milford be paid L2 2s 4d of the proceeds and balance be returned to the Jurisdiction treasurer. It's unknown when James was released from prison. In 1668, he was to be in East Hampton with his parents. On 22 June 1668, he was part of the successful party in a minor lawsuit. In 1671, he was in New Haven, perhaps involved in shipping and was complained of, "for making the people muse [i.e. wander] with strange storyes & bragging what he could do. He being examined before the Deputy governor & James Bishop & being convicted of lyeing, was fined Ten shillings, and the Constables ordered to receive it of him." He married Elizabeth Gardiner Howell in 1674. He made a grant of L100 of his estate to his wife, and "after her to her children by me begotten" and also appointed guardians, or trustees "in behalf of my wife and child or children." On 26 March 1678, he made a trust for his father-in-law and his wife and her heirs "one Indian captive girl, about 14 years old, called 'Beck.'" In 1682-3, he was a partner with his uncles Jacob and Isaac and others in a venture to recover a plate from a Spanish wreck on the Bahama Islands. His is listed on a tax list of East Hampton of 8 September 1683. On 4 September 1686, his signature on his own will was testified by Nathaniel Baker. He died before 7 April 1686. Elizabeth was alive on 28 March 1683 as she was mentioned in her father's will.

    i.   Joanne
    ii.   Arthur
    iii. Lion

JOHANNA LOPER, bapt. as "Janneken" on 30 October 1650 Dutch Church, Jochem Pietersen [Kuyter], Janneken Molyns and Marritje Jacobs were witnesses; (M1) Joris "George" Christoffelse Davids/Davidsen on 9 December 1674 at Dutch Church; Joris was familiar with the language of the Esopus Indians; Joris d. before 30 December 1680 (M2) Hendricus Beekman.

Johanna (M1) Joris

    i.   Jacobua/Jacob
    ii.   Samuel
    iii. Solomon Sr.

Johanna (M2) Hendricus

This branch published through:

http://iment.com/maida/familytree/ henry/bios/hendrickbeekman.htm.

Jacobus Schellinger and Cornelia Melyn **WILLIAM SCHELLINGER**, b. March 1654; d. 6 March 1735, East Hampton, New York.

CATHARINE/CATALYNTJE SCHELLINGER, b. 9 April 1656 New Amsterdam, New York; m. Nathaniel Baker about 1677; d. 18 May 1722 East Hampton, New York; buried Amagansett, New York, Old Burying Ground.

    i.   Lt. Jonathan
    ii.   Joanna
    iii. Abigail
    iv. Henry
    v.   Catherine
    vi. Mary
    vii. Daniel
    viii. Hanna

JACOBUS SCHELLINGER, b. 1663, East Hampton, New York; m. Hannah Hicks 1690; d. 28 January 1712 East Hampton, New York.

    i.   Hannah
    ii.   Catherine
    iii. Hester
    iv. Mercy
    v.   Jacob
    vi. Abigail
    vii. Daniel
    viii. Daniel
    ix. Jonathan

ABRAHAM SCHELLINGER, b. 11 February 1659 New Haven, Connecticut; Whaler on Long Island; (M1)

Joanna Hedges 15 November 1688 East Hampton, New York; (M2) Philipa Hathaway; d. 1 January 1712 Amagansett, New York.

Abraham (M1) Joanna

- i.   Johanna
- ii.   Rachel
- iii. William
- iv. Abraham
- v.   Isaac
- vi. Amy
- vii. Zerviah

DANIEL LOPER SCHELLINGER, b. 19 July 1665 New Amsterdam, New York; m. ?; d. leaving a widow, 1701 Batavia, Dutch East Indies.

CORNELIUS SCHELLINGER, b. 1668 East Hampton, New York

GENERATION II

James Loper and Elizabeth Howell

Arthur Loper

Lion Loper

Joanna Loper

Johanna Loper (M1) Joris Davids

JACOBUS/JACOB DAVIDS, christened 17 November 1675 Kingston, New York.

SAMUEL DAVIDS, christened 26 May 1678 Kingston, New York.

SOLOMON DAVIDS SR., b. 25 March 1680 Kingston, New York; Indian trader in Machackemeck along Delaware and Susquehanna; not married to Beletje Quick; d. after May 1738 Sussex, New Jersey.

    i.   Solomon Jr.
    ii.   Joel Quick

*Catharine Schellinger and
Nathaniel Baker*

LT. JONATHAN BAKER, b. 12 February 1679 Elizabethtown, New Jersey.

JOANNA BAKER, b. 7 July 1681; m. Joseph Ogden 1704; d. 26 May 1714.

    i.   Joanna

    ii.   Joseph
    iii. Daniel
    iv. Nathaniel

ABIGAIL BAKER, b. 15 March 1682 Elizabethtown, New Jersey.

HENRY BAKER

CATHERINE BAKER, b. 4 April 1687 Elizabethtown, New Jersey.

MARY BAKER, b. 21 November 1688 Elizabethtown, New Jersey; d. 1725.

DANIEL BAKER, b. 1 August 1692 East Hampton, New York; m. Abigail Osborn 7 September 1714 East Hampton, New York; d. 16 March 1740 East Hampton, New York.

    i.   Daniel
    ii.   Nathaniel
    iii. (?)
    iv. Elizabeth
    v.   Henry
    vi. Abraham
    vii. Abigail

HANNA BAKER

Jacob Schellinger and Hannah Hicks

HANNAH SCHELLINGER, b. 15 August 1693 East Hampton, New York; m. William Whitehead 3 May 1715.

CATHERINE SCHELLINGER, b. 5 August
1695 East Hampton, New York; m.
John Conkling Jr. 1725.

  i.   Meylan
  ii. Jonathan
  iii. Daniel
  iv. Katherine

HESTER SCHELLINGER, b. 16 November
1697 East Hampton, New York;
m. Thomas Osborne 8 December
1720.

  i.   Jacob
  ii.   (?)
  iii. Esther
  iv.   Mary
  v.   Keturah
  vi.   Stephen
  vii. (?)
  viii. (?)
  ix.   (?)

MERCY SCHELLINGER, b. 11 April
1699 East Hampton, New York; m.
Samuel Baker 18 October 1721.

  i.   Mercy
  ii. Hannah
  iii. Esther
  iv. Samuel
  v.   Jonathan

JACOB SCHELLINGER, b. 22 November
1701 East Hampton, New York; m.
Elisheba Miller 19 May 1724 East
Hampton, New York; d. 10 January
1753 East Hampton, New York.

  i.   Hannah
  ii.   Jacob
  iii. Mary
  iv.   Mercy
  v.   Jonathan
  vi.   Catherine
  vii. Abraham
  viii. Isaac
  ix.   Esther
  x.   Daniel

ABIGAIL SCHELLINGER, b. 14 February
1703/04 East Hampton, New York; m.
William Rogers 12 November 1724.

DANIEL SCHELLINGER, b. 13 June
1708 East Hampton, New York; d.
before 28 March 1709.

DANIEL SCHELLINGER, b. 1 March
1708/09 East Hampton, New York;
d. 1785 Morris, New Jersey.

JONATHAN SCHELLINGER, b. 12
December 1712 East Hampton, New
York; d. 18 March 1718/19.

Abraham Schellinger (M1)
Joanna Hedges

JOHANNA SCHELLINGER, b. 7 July 1689
East Hampton, New York; m. Samuel
Ogden; d. 13 September 1775.

RACHEL SCHELLINGER, b. 8 November
1691; d. 16 December 1744.

WILLIAM SCHELLINGER, b. 9 April
1694; d. 24 February 1718.

ABRAHAM SCHELLINGER, b. 20 June 1697; d. 6 October 1718.

ISAAC SCHELLINGER, b. 17 March 1699; d. 1 December 1769.

AMY SCHELLINGER, b. 17 June 1701.

ZERVIAH SCHELLINGER, b. 15 August 1705 Amagansett, New York; m. Samuel Hudson 9 November 1722 East Hampton, New York; d. Mendham, New Jersey.

i.	Samuel
ii.	Abraham
iii.	Zerviah
iv.	(?)
v.	(?)
vi.	Joanna
vii.	William

GENERATION III

Soloman Davids Sr. and Beletje Quick

SOLOMAN DAVIDS JR., christened 1711 Kingston, New York; m. Leah Decker 1733 Orange, New York; d. before 20 October 1752.

i. Lea
ii. Jacobus
iii. Beletje/Isabella
iv. Daniel
v. Joel
vi. Jonas
vii. Catherine
viii. Elisabeth
ix. Petrus
x. Solomon
xi. Son
xii. Daughter

JOEL QUICK, christened 16 January 1726 Kingston, New York; m. Christina Middagh.

i. Beletje

Joanna Baker and Joseph Ogden

JOANNA OGDEN, b. 2 June 1706; (M1) John Meeker; (M2) John Alling; d. 22 April 1761.

Joanna and Meeker

i. John
ii. Joanna
iii. Rebecca
iv. Mary
v. Hannah
vi. Phebe

Joanna and Alling

vii. Eunice

JOSEPH OGDEN, b. 1709; m. Esther Conklin; d. 29 April 1761.

DANIEL OGDEN SR., b. 22 April 1761; m. Mary.

i. Timothy
ii. Daniel Jr.

NATHANIEL OGDEN, b. 1713; m. Judith Bouquett (Bonquett); d. 12 October 1790.

i. Samuel
ii. James
iii. David
iv. Pvt. John
v. Phebe
vi. Pvt. Benjamin

Daniel Baker and Abigail Osborn

DANIEL BABER, b. 1715 East Hampton, New York.

NATHANIEL BAKER, b. 1718 East Hampton, New York

(?) BAKER, b. December 1720 East Hampton, New York

ELIZABETH BAKER, b. about 1721 East Hampton, New York

HENRY BAKER, b. about 1727 East Hampton, New York; m. Phebe Hedges 1750 East Hampton, New York; d. 13 May 1780 Westfield, New Jersey.

    i.   Daniel

ABRAHAM BAKER, b. about 1729 East Hampton, New York

ABIGAIL BAKER, b. about 1732 East Hampton, New York

Catherine Schellinger and John Conkling

MEYLAN MALINES CONKLING, christened 25 August 1728 East Hampton, New York.

JONATHAN CONKLING, christened 14 March 1729/30.

DANIEL CONKLING, christened 11 January 1735/36.

KATHERINE CONKLING, b. about 1732; m. Culpepper Frisbie 1758.

Hester Schellinger and Thomas Osborne

JACOB OSBORN, bapt. 17 December 1721 East Hampton, New York; m. Amy (Anne) Stratton December 1746 East Hampton, New York; d. 19 January 1792 Amagansett, New York.

    i.   Esther
    ii.   Thomas
    iii.   (?)
    iv.   (?)
    v.   (?)
    vi.   Philetus
    vii. Jacob
    viii. child
    ix.   Smith Stratton
    x.   (?)
    xi.   Ame
    xii. child
    xiii. Elizabeth

ESTHER OSBORN, b. 8 December 1723; bapt. 8 September 1723 East Hampton, New York; d. 16 January 1739/40 East Hampton, New York; buried Amagansett, New York.

MARY OSBORN, b./bapt. 9 November 1729 East Hampton, New York.

KETURAH OSBORN, b. 27 May 1733; bapt. 27 November 1733 East Hampton, New York; d. 21 February 1790.

STEPHEN OSBORN, b./bapt. 20 June 1736 East Hampton, New York; m. Margret Hoel 17 February 1777 Hanover, New Jersey; d. 1794.

(?) OSBORN, d. 19 July 1766 East Hampton, New York.

    i.   Elias
   ii.   Esther

(?) OSBORN, d. 15 march 1776 Hanover, New Jersey.

(?) OSBORN, (M3) Margaret Howell 17 February 1777.

(?) OSBORN, (M2) Timothy Mulford 1803 Morris County, New Jersey.

Mercy Schellinger and Samuel Baker

MERCY BAKER

HANNAH BAKER

ESTHER BAKER

SAMUEL BAKER

JONATHAN BAKER

Jacob Schellinger and Elisheba Miller
HANNAH SCHELLINGER, b. 1725 East Hampton, New York; m. Joseph Hicks

10 November 1745 East Hampton, New York; d. Long Island, New York.

    i.   Elizabeth
   ii.   Zacheriah
  iii.   Jacob
  iv.   Lydia
   v.   Hannah
  vi.   Daniel
 vii.   Ruth
viii.   Mary
  ix.   Joseph

JACOB SCHELLINGER, b. 1727 East Hampton, New York; d. 2 May 1751 East Hampton, New York.

MARY SCHELLINGER, b. 1729 East Hampton, New York; m. David Daniel 1754 East Hampton, New York; d. After 1745 East Hampton, New York.

MERCY SCHELLINGER, b. 1729 East Hampton, New York; m. Zebedee Osborn 1 February 1750/51.

    i.   Abigail
   ii.   Abraham
  iii.   Elisha
  iv.   Ruth

JONATHAN SCHELLINGER, b. 1730 East Hampton, New York; d. 4 June 1814 East Hampton, New York.

CATHERINE SCHELLINGER, b. 1736 East Hampton, New York; m. Jacob Conkling.

ABRAHAM SCHELLINGER, b. 10 September 1738 East Hampton, New York; m. Lois Conkling.

ISAAC SCHELLINGER, b. 1741 East Hampton, New York.

ESTHER SCHELLINGER, b. 1741.

DANIEL SCHELLINGER, b. 1744 East Hampton, New York.

*Zervia Schellinger and
Samuel Hudson*

SAMUEL HUDSON JR., b. 30 January 1724 East Hampton, New York; m. Mary Mulford; d. 1755 Morristown, New Jersey.

ABRAHAM HUDSON, b. 17 February 1726.

ZERVIAH HUDSON, b. 7 March 1728 East Hampton, New York.

(?) HUDSON, b. about 1732; d. about 1732.

(?) HUDSON, b. about 1732; d. about 1732.

JOANNA HUDSON, b. 11 November 1733 East Hampton, New York.

WILLIAM HUDSON, b. 26 September 1736 East Hampton, New York.

GENERATION IV

Solomon Davids and Leah Decker

LEA DAVIDS, christened 18 June 1734 Machackemeck, New York.

JACOBUS DAVIDS, christened 18 May 1736 Machackemeck, New York.

BELETJE/ISABELLA DAVIDS, b. Upper Smithfield, Pennsylvania; christened 31 May 1738 Machackemeck, New York; m. Jacob Figley III 28 July 1758 Machackemeck, New York; d. after 14 March 1821 Union, Pennsylvania.

    i.   Simeon
    ii.   Zachariah
    iii. Adam
    iv. Eve (Eva)
    v.   Jonas
    vi. Abraham
    vii. Jacob III
    viii. Mary
    ix. Elizabeth
    x.   Joseph
    xi. Margaret

DANIEL DAVIDS, christened 18 June 1740 Machackemeck, New York.

JOEL DAVIDS, christened 23 April 1744 Machackemeck, New York

JONAS DAVIDS, christened 16 June 1745 Machackemeck, New York

CATHERINE DAVIDS, christened 21 June 1747 Machackemeck, New York

ELISABETH DAVIDS, christened 20 March 1748 Machackemeck, New York.

PETRUS DAVIDS, christened 15 April 1750 Machackemeck, New York.

SOLOMON DAVIDS JR., christened 5 April 1752 Machackemeck, New York.

(MALE) DAVIDS, b. about 1754.

(DAUGHTER) DAVIDS, b. about 1756.

Joel Quick and Christina Middagh

BELETJE QUICK, christened 26 August 1759 New York.

Joanna Ogden and John Meeker

JOANNA MEEKER, m. Nathan Baldwin.

REBECCA MEEKER, b. 1726; m. David Squire.

MARY MEEKER, b. 1728; d. 13 February 1768; m. Amos Potter.

HANNAH MEEKER, m. Samuel Hicks.

PHEBE MEEKER, m. Steven Meeker (her second cousin).

JOHN MEEKER, b. 1731; d. March 1768

Joanna Ogden and John Alling

EUNIS ALLING.

Daniel Ogden Sr. and Mary

TIMOTHY OGDEN, b. 5 April 1781; m. Hannah Chapman (?).

 i. Mary
 ii. Ichabod
 iii. William
 iv. Moses
 v. Joseph

DANIEL OGDEN III, b. 14 April 1737; d. 6 December 1809.

Nathaniel Ogden and
Judith Bouquett

SAMUEL OGDEN

JAMES OGDEN

DAVID OGDEN, b. 1741.

PVT. JOHN OGDEN, b. 1743.

PHEBE OGDEN, b. 22 October 1749.

PVT. BENJAMIN OGDEN, b. 27 October 1751; d. 1 February 1790.

Henry Baker and Phebe Hedges

DANIEL BAKER, b. 3 June 1753 New Jersey; m. Margaret Osborn; d. 10 July 1814.

 i. Mary
 ii. David
 iii. Phebe
 iv. Margaret
 v. Daniel
 vi. Elizabeth
 vi. Daniel
 vii. Hedges
 viii. Prudence
 ix. Cyrus
 x. Henry
 xi. Hannah
 xii. Elihu
 xiii. Electra

(male) Osborn and
Amy (Anne) Stratton

ESTHER OSBORN, b. September 1747; (M2) Timothy Mulford; d. 21 July 1803; buried Presbyterian Churchyard, Hanover, New Jersey.

THOMAS OSBORN, b. 16 April 1750 New York; d. 5 April 1804; buried Presbyterian churchyard, New Providence, New Jersey.

(?) OSBORN, (M1) Lois Ellison; d. 18 January 1783 New Jersey.

 i. Elizabeth
 ii. Smith Stratton

(?) OSBORN, (M2) Rachel Roff 15 may 1783 New Jersey.

(?) OSBORN, (M3) Col. Jedediah Swan; d. Scotch Plains, New Jersey.

PHILETUS OSBORN, b. 1752; d. 30 April 1830; m. Hannah; buried Amagansett Cemetery, New York.

JACOB OSBORN, b. 1755; m. Elizabeth Dalglish; d. 1 February 1808.

(CHILD) OSBORN, b. 1757; d. 29 June 1757.

SMITH STRATTON OSBORN, b. 11 March 1759 Amagansett, New York; m. Sarah Burnet; d. 25 April 1816 New Jersey; buried Presbyterian churchyard, New Jersey.

(?) OSBORN, m. Sarah Burnet; d. 15 September 1841 New Jersey.

    i.   Esther
    ii.   Stephen
    iii. Hannah
    iv. Jacob
    v.   Stratton
    vi. Ellis
    vii. Esrael Day

AME OSBORN, b. 1761; m. Nathan Beers; d. 8 October 1837.

(CHILD) OSBORN, b. 1763; d. November 1763.

ELIZABETH OSBORN, b. 8 December 1766; m. David Dayton.

(?) Osborn and (?)

ELIAS

ESTHER

Hannah Schellinger and Joseph Hicks

ELIZABETH HICKS, b. 1746 East Hampton, New York.

ZACHERIAH HICKS, b. 1749 East Hampton, New York.

JACOB HICKS b. 1752 East Hampton, New York; m. Betsy Hand.

LYDIA HICKS, b. 1754 East Hampton, New York.

HANNAH HICKS, b. 1756 East Hampton, New York.

DANIEL BISHOP HICKS, b. 26 December 1759 East Hampton, New York; m. Mary Williams Sill; d. 8 July 1847 Fleming, New York.

RUTH HICKS, b. 1762 East Hampton, New York; d. 1771 East Hampton, New York.

MARY HICKS, b. 1764 East Hampton, New York

JOSEPH HICKS, b. 1766 East Hampton, New York; d. 1784 East Hampton, New York.

*Mercy Schellinger and
Zebedee Osborn*

ABIGAIL OSBORN, b. January 1753 East Hampton, New York; m. About 1775 John Norris.

ABRAHAM OSBORN, b. about 1756 East Hampton, New York.

ELISHA OSBORN, b. About 1761 East Hampton, New York; m. Sarah Osborn.

RUTH OSBORN, b. 4 February 1759 East Hampton, New York; d. 3 July 1775.

GENERATION V

*Beletje/Isabella Davids and
Jacob Figley III*

SIMEON FIGLEY, b. before 28 January 1759 Sussex, New Jersey; m. Agnes; d. after 29 July 1819 Shelby, Kentucky

ZACHARIAH FIGLEY, b. before 20 March 1761 Sussex, New Jersey; d. 10 May 1853 Hopewell, Pennsylvania.

ADAM FIGLEY, b. before 22 May 1763 Sussex, New Jersey; m. Elizabeth Guthrie.

EVE (EVA) FIGLEY, b. Sussex, New Jersey; christened 28 October 1765 Machackemeck, New York; m. Matthew Myers about 1785 Pennsylvania; d. 13 January 1861 Steubenville, Ohio.

    i.   John
    ii. Abraham
    iii. Elizabeth/Betsy
    iv. Joseph
    v.   Mary
    vi. Margaret
    vii. Matthew
    viii. James
    ix. William
    x.   Nancy

JONAS FIGLEY, b. 31 July 1767 Pennsylvania; m. Elizabeth; d. 11 August 1855 York, Ohio.

ABRAHAM FIGLEY b. 1769; m. Catharine Donelson; d. 3 September 1834 Columbiana, Ohio.

JACOB FIGLEY III, b. 2 March 1771 Pennsylvania; m. Agnes; d. 11 December 1858 Union, Pennsylvania

MARY FIGLEY, b. 23 July 1776 Pennsylvania; d. 26 November 1838 Union, Pennsylvania.

ELIZABETH FIGLEY, b. between 1777 and 1779 Pennsylvania.

JOSEPH FIGLEY b. 1780 Pennsylvania; m. Jemima Castner; d. 7 July 1860 Hanover, Ohio.

MARGARET FIGLEY, b. 1782 Washington, Pennsylvania; m. Samuel Lafferty 1 January 1807; d. 4 April 1842.

    i.   Belijah
    ii. Jacob
    iii. Edward
    iv. Elizabeth
    v.   Jane
    vi. Joseph
    vii. Margaret

*Timothy Ogden and Hannah
Chapman (?)*

MARY OGDEN

Ichabod Ogden

William Ogden, b. 1766.

Moses Ogden, b. 6 February 1774; d. 9 June 1847.

Joseph G. Ogden, b. 1780.

Daniel Baker and Margaret Osborn

Mary Baker

David Baker

Phebe Baker

Margaret Baker

Daniel Baker

Elizabeth Baker

Daniel Baker

Hedges Baker

Prudence Baker

Cyrus Baker

Henry Baker

Hannah Baker

Elihu Baker

Electra Baker

(male) Osborn and Lois Ellison

Elizabeth Osborn, d. 22 November 1848.

Smith Stratton Osborn, d. 29 September 1806.

(male) Osborn and Sarah Burnet

Esther Osborn, b. 1782; d. 15 October 1805.

Stephen Burnet Osborn, d. 22 October 1844.

Hannah Osborn

Jacob Osborn

Stratton Osborn

Ellis Osborn

Israel Day Osborn, d. After 1852.

(male) Osborne and (?)

Elias Conkling Osborne, b. 27 March 1763; d. After 1828.

Esther Osborne, b. 1764.

Mariken "Maria" Melyn

Mariken was born and baptized as "Meriken" on 27 March 1637 by Doctor Trelcatius, which was witnessed by Christian Melijn in Nieuwe Kerk, Amsterdam. She came to New Netherland with her parents in 1641. She (M1) Claes Allertsen Parakijs on 18 June 1655, but he was later killed in the Indian Massacre of September 1655.

New Haven, Connecticut

Maria went to New Haven with her parents in 1655 where she would (M2) "Matthias Hitfield" on 25 August 1664, which was performed by "Mr. Wm. Jones," which was a double wedding as her sister, Susanna, was also being married to John Winans at the same time. About 1665, they moved to the newly settled plantation on the Arthur Cull sound, Elizabeth Town, New Jersey where "Matthias Heathfield," with sixty-two others, is subscribed to the "Oath of Aleagance & Fidelety" taken on 19 February 1665, therefore founding Elizabeth Town. He was a weaver and a boatman, a man of considerable means. In a record of surveys at Elizabeth of 29 August 1676, he is called "Hatfield" and in his will, "Hattfield." His house lot contained five acres and he had in addition twenty-two acres of upland "in a triangle," twelve acres of land, one hundred and twelve acres of upland, forty acres of upland, seventeen acres of meadow, for a total of two hundred and eight acres. On 5 December 1673, he bought a stone house on Pearl Street at the corner of Hatafield, from Mr. Lubberson. This remained in the family until 1914 (241 years), "For twelve hundred guilders secured to him by bill" (a large sum in those days) of "Abraham Lubberson of New Orania in the New Netherlands, his dwelling house and lott with all other accommodations belonging to a first lott within the bounds of Elizabeth both upland and meadow". The property from the stone house extended to the Elizabeth River where he had tanneries. He gave land for the Presbyterian Church in 1677 and burial ground (which is now the center of town). Alexander Hamilton used to walk there learning his lessons while attending school at Barbers. In a deed acknowledged before Philip Carteret on 25 October 1677, Maria signed her name "Heatfield," even when he signs as "Heathfield". He was treated in New Haven by Dr. John Winthrop, Jr. (also governor) who made an entry about him in his medical records:

> *Hetfield Mathias an high duchman of Dantsick now living at New haven hath paine in knee & swolled: hath used muche meanes to purghe him by direction of a swiddish skipper: discharge enough way to have finished it in couple days but it returns worse. I gave him 5 doz 15 gr & 4 doz 3 gr: addib. Because he said he had some 8 gr m 7 Dabaus: & nnot workd also he had pl both.*

Mathias was one of the leading men in town and greatly respected. He sat in the Justices Court as a chosen Freeholder. He was also a Justice, High Sheriff, and a Collector for the County. He died on 13 December 1687 in New Haven, Connecticut or Elizabethtown, New Jersey. His will dated on 19 April 1684, and was proven on 13 December 1687 only mentioned, "wife and children," but not named. Mariken was living in 1694, when her name appears on the Parish List of the Independent Minister.

Mariken and Claes Allertsen:
i.   Claes Paradys

Mariken and Matthias:
ii. Isaac
iii. Cornelius

iv.   Mary
v.   George Abraham Sr.
vi.   Rachel
vii. Mary
viii. Elizabeth

GENERATION I

Claes Allertsen Parakijs and Mariken Melyn

CLAES PARADYS, bapt. 3 November 1655 in Dutch Church, Jacobus Schellinger and Cornelia Melyn were sponsors.

Matthias Hatfield and Mariken Melyn

ISAAC HATFIELD, b. 1665 New Haven, Connecticut; m. Sarah Melyn; d. 1762.

    i.   Sarah
    ii.   Abigail
    iii. Isaac
    iv. Benjamin
    v.   Moses
    vi. Andrew
    vii. Pheobe

CORNELIUS HATFIELD, b. 1666 New York City, New York; bapt. 9 June 1669 in Dutch Church with Jannetje Molyn as witness; his father's surname was given as "Sircrel"; 21 March 1689/90 he joined with his mother in deeding some property of what was formerly his father's; he purchased land from Col. Richard Towney in 1690 in Elizabeth Town, which adjoined his brother Isaac Hatfield; was a cordwainer and tanner at Elizabeth; (M1) Abigail before 1691 and (M2) Sarah Price 1691; 10 September 1700, had party

of 60 citizens, including himself, his brothers Abraham and Isaac and other descendants of Cornelius Melyn, rescued Samuel Burwell from the Court of Sessions at Newark. This was the sequel to a remonstrance against the acts of the Proprietors of East Jersey, which had been made by the same persons a few days earlier. On this date, Abraham Hatfield pulled the Presiding Justice, William Sanford, from the bench and knocked off his hat and wig. The other Justices were also abused and the Constable set upon. Cornelius' will was dated on 17 May 1718 and proved on 14 August which named him a yeoman, and mentioned his wife, Sarah, his son Cornelius (under 21) also one married and five unmarried daughters. One item in the inventory of 31 December 1718 was a "great English bible"; died 22 May 1718 in Elizabeth, New Jersey; buried St. John's churchyard as his tombstone states that he was in his 52nd year.

Cornelius and Sarah

    i.   Anna
    ii.   Sarah
    iii. Mary
    iv. Rachel
    v.   Elizabeth
    vi. Cornelius
    vii. Joanna

MARY HATFIELD, b. 1668 Elizabethtown, New Jersey; m. Richard Miller; d. 17 December 1742.

GEORGE ABRAHAM HATFIELD, SR., b. Elizabeth, New Jersey; bapt. 8 June 1670 New York Dutch Reformed Church with Jannetje Molyn as sponsor; m. Phoebe Ogden about 1695; bred a cordwainer and ran a tannery with brother, Cornelius; boatman and farmer; involved with his brother, Cornelius, in attack on Justices at Newark in 1700; chosen as associate in 1693, signer of a petition to the King, purporting to be from "The Freeholders Inhabitants and owners of land of and belonging to Elizabethtown or township in the Province of East New Jersey in America.'" Made his will on 8 July 1706; proven 23 July 1706; Phoebe's maiden name been variously given as Lyon, Ogden and Woodruff; d. 17 July 1706 in Trenton, New Jersey.

i. George Jr.
ii. Matthias
iii. Joseph
iv. Jacob
v. Susanne
vi. Mary

RACHEL HATFIELD, bapt. 3 October 1674 Dutch Reformed Church, New York; according to Anne Chaney (from James Hatfield), Rachel was twin to Abraham.

MARY HATFIELD, b. 1674 Elizabethtown, New Jersey; m. Richard Miller.

ELIZABETH HATFIELD, b. 1676 Elizabethtown, New Jersey; m. Maximillian LaLour 1708 Essex, New Jersey; d. 28 September 1725.

GENERATION II

Isaac Hatfield I and Sarah Melyn

SARAH HATFIELD, b. 1728 Elizabeth, New Jersey; m. her cousin, Abraham Clark (son of Thomas Clark and Hannah Winans, Susanna Melyn descendants), signer of Declaration of Independence; d. 2 June 1804 Middlesex, New Jersey.

    i.   Sarah
    ii.   Thomas
    iii. Aaron
    iv. Abraham
    v.   Hannah
    vi. Elizabeth
    vii. Andrew
    viii. Cavalier
    ix. Abraham Jr.
    x.   Abigail

ABIGAIL HATFIELD, b. Elizabethtown, New Jersey; m. Chevalier Jouet; d. 22 February 1770.

    i.   Elizabeth
    ii.   John
    iii. Daniel
    iv. Susanna
    v.   Xenophon
    vi. Sarah
    vii. Mary

ISAAC HATFIELD, b. 1750; an elder in Presbyterian Church; m. Sarah Price; owned a race course on Halstead Point Road; advertised in New York papers; d. 1807.

    i.   Phebe
    ii.   Jout
    iii. Aaron
    iv. Benjamin
    v.   Abigail
    vi. Moses
    vii. Andrew
    viii. Sarah
    ix. Isaac

BENJAMIN HATFIELD, b. 1753 Elizabethtown, New Jersey; m. Anne Merrill 10 January 1765 St. Andrew's, Steuben, New York; d. January 1783 New Jersey.

    i.   John
    ii.   Jane

MOSES HATFIELD, b. 21 April 1755 Elizabethtown, New Jersey; m. Abigail Harriman 1774 Camden, New Jersey; d. 14 April 1803 Elizabethtown, New Jersey.

    i.   Abigail
    ii.   John
    iii. James
    iv. Sarah
    v.   Job H.
    vi. Abigail

vii. Edward D.
viii. Hannah Miller
ix.   Moses

ANDREW HATFIELD, b. 1758 Elizabethtown, New Jersey; m. Mary Price 1762; d. 19 January 1824 Westfield, New Jersey.

i.   Abigail
ii.   Phebe
iii. Sarah
iv.   Mary
v.   Jacob
vi.   Andrew
vii. Elizabeth
viii. Hannah
ix.   John
x.   Phebe
xi.   Baker
xii. Margaret
xiii. Margaret
xiv. Abraham

PHEOBE HATFIELD, b. 1760 Elizabethtown, New Jersey; m. Baker Hendricks; d. 9 January 1779 New Jersey.

i.   Hannah
ii.   Hannah
iii. John
iv.   Phebe
v.   Baker
vi.   Margaret
vii. Margaret
viii. Abraham

Cornelius Hatfield and Sarah Price

ANNA RACHEL HATFIELD, b. 1694-5 Elizabeth-town, New Jersey; m. Jeremiah/ Joseph Ludlum before 17 May 1718; d. 1765.

i.   Cornelius
ii.   Matthias
iii. Ann

SARAH HATFIELD, b. about 1701 Elizabethtown, New Jersey; m. John Peter Salnave February 1724.

i.   Hannay
ii.   Elizabeth
iii. Magdalen
iv.   Phoebe
v.   Ann
vi.   Peter
vii. Sarah

MARY HATFIELD, b. 1703 Elizabeth, New Jersey; m. Cornelius Badgley; d. 9 August 1794.

i.   George
ii.   Cornelius
iii. Elizabeth
iv.   Sarah
v.   Mary
vi.   Rachel

RACHEL MARY HATFIELD, b. 1703 Elizabethtown, New Jersey; m. George Badgley Sr. 1717; buried Presbyterian Church, New Jersey.

i. Hannah
ii. George
iii. Cornelius
iv. Sarah
v. Nancy
vi. Mary
vii. Elizabeth
viii. Rachel

ELIZABETH HATFIELD, b. 1704-7 Elizabethtown, New Jersey; m. Aaron Miller.

i. Nancy
ii. Elizabeth
iii. Aaron
iv. Cornelius
v. Robert
vi. Phebe

CORNELIUS HATFIELD II, b. 1709-10 Elizabeth-town, New Jersey; m. Abigail Price; Deacon, slave trader, merchant and store owner; d. 20 March 1795.

i. Ann
ii. Joanna
iii. Abner
iv. Cornelius III
v. Abigail
vi. Caleb

JOANNA HATFIELD, b. 13 November 1714 Elizabethtown, New Jersey; d. 12 April 1723.

George Hatfield Sr. and
Phoebe Ogden

GEORGE ABRAHAM HATFIELD JR., b. 1695 Elizabeth, New Jersey; m. Margaret Winans 1716 New Jersey; tanner; d. 1742-5 Elizabethtown, New Jersey; will dated 16 October 1742 and proved 4 May 1745.

i. Joseph Sr.
ii. Jeremiah
iii. George
iv. Abraham
v. John David
vi. Sarah
vii. Samuel
viii. Elias
ix. Jacob
x. Phoebe
xi. Susan
xii. William
xiii. Matthias

MATTHIAS HATFIELD, b. 1697 Elizabethtown, New Jersey; m. Hannah Miller about January 1720; d. 10 December 1779; will dated 15 September 1779, proved 5 November 1783; headstone reads "Deacon Matthias Hatfield."

i. Phoebe
ii. Hannah
iii. Matthias
iv. Aaron

v.   Matthias
vi.   Elizabeth
vii. Jonathan
viii. Moses

JOSEPH HATFIELD, b. 1700 Elizabethtown, New Jersey; m. Phoebe Clark; d. 1793.

i.   Mary Ann

JACOB HATFIELD, b. about 1702 Elizabethtown, New Jersey; (M1) Mary 1722; (M2) Esther Thomas 1710.

Jacob and Mary

i.   James

Jacob and Esther

i.   Abraham
ii.   Margaret
iii. Lydia

ELIAS HATFIELD, b. Elizabethtown, New Jersey.

SUSANNE HATFIELD, b. 1697 Elizabethtown, New Jersey; m. Peter Decker; d. Staten Island, New York.

i.   Maria
ii.   Johannes
iii. Susanna
iv.   Peter
v.   Sarah
vi.   Mattheus
vii. Eva
viii. Abraham
ix.   Jacob

MARY HATFIELD, b. about 1705 Rahway, New Jersey; m. Henry Baker; d. 13 April 1755; buried Rahway, New Jersey.

i.   Mary
ii.   (child)
iii. Susanna
iv.   Henry
v.   Jacob
vi.   Cornelius
vii. Matthias
viii. William

ISAAC HATFIELD, b. Elizabeth, New Jersey.

GENERATION III

Abraham Clark and Sarah Hatfield

AARON CLARK, b. 1750 Rahway, New Jersey; m. Susanna Winans; d. 1811/2 Washington County, Pennsylvania.

    i.   Winans
    ii.   Elizabeth
    iii. Hatfield
    iv. Josiah
    v.   Hannah
    vi. Abigail
    vii. Susannah

THOMAS CLARK, b. 1753 Rahway, New Jersey; m. Elizabeth Dixon 1775; d. 13 May 1789 Rahway, New Jersey.

    i.   Jonathan
    ii.   David
    iii. Abraham

ABRAHAM CLARK, b. 1755; d. 26 July 1758.

HANNAH CLARK, b. 1755; m. Melyn Miller after 11 August 1777; d. 8 November 1830.

ANDREW CLARK, b. 1761 Elizabethtown, New Jersey.

SARAH CLARK, b. 1761 Elizabethtown, New Jersey; m. Clarkson Edgar; d. 2 October 1817.

    i.   Henrietta
    ii.   Abraham

ELIZABETH CLARK.

ABRAHAM CLARK, b. 2 October 1767 Elizabeth-town, New Jersey; (M1) Hannah Perkins; (M2) Lydia Griffith; d. 28 July 1854 Kinderhook, New York.

Abraham and Lydia

    i.   Eliza

CAVALIER CLARK, b. 1763; d. 4 November 1764.

ABIGAIL CLARK, b. 1773 Elizabethtown, New Jersey; m. Thomas Salter 28 October 1802; d. 25 October 1811.

    i.   George
    ii.   Louisa

Cavalier Jouet and Abigail Hatfield

ELIZABETH JOUET.

JOHN TROUP JOUET, Revolutionary War New Jersey Volunteer.

DANIEL JOUET, m. Gilmore (?).

SUSANNA JOUET, m. Alexander Cameron.

XENOPHON JOUET, b. 1760; m.
Gertrude Garretson 28 August 1783;
d. 1843.

    i.   Abigail
    ii. Sarah
    iii. Susan
    iv. Cavalier
    v.   Thomas
    vi. Ann
    vii. John
    viii. Gertrude
    ix. Beverly
    x.   Isaac

SARAH JOUET, b. 1764; m. Jacob
Dehart.

    i.   John
    ii. Mary
    iii. Eliza
    iv. Sarah

MARY JOUET, b. 22 July 1765; m.
Aaron Dayton October 1800.

Isaac Hatfield and Sarah Price

PHEBE HATFIELD.

JOUT HATFIELD.

AARON HATFIELD.

BENJAMIN HATFIELD.

ABIGIAL HATFIELD.

MOSES HATFIELD.

ANDREW HATFIELD.

SARAH HATFIELD, b. 1728 Elizabeth,
New Jersey; m. Abraham Clark, signer
of Declaration of Independence; d. 2
June 1804 New Jersey.

ISAAC HATFIELD.

Benjamin Hatfield and Anne Merrill

JOHN HATFIELD.

JANE HATFIELD.

*Moses Hatfield and
Abigail Harriman*

ABIGAIL HATFIELD.

JOHN HATFIELD.

JAMES CALDWELL HATFIELD.

SARAH HATFIELD.

JOB HATFIELD.

EDWARD HATFIELD.

HANNAH HATFIELD.

MOSES HATFIELD.

Andrew Hatfield and Mary Price

ABIGAIL HATFIELD.

PHEBE HATFIELD.

SARAH HATFIELD.

MARY HATFIELD.

JACOB HATFIELD.

ANDREW HATFIELD.

ELIZABETH HATFIELD.

HANNAH HATFIELD.

JOHN HATFIELD.

PHEBE HATFIELD.

BAKER HATFIELD.

MARGARET HATFIELD.

MARGARET HATFIELD.

ABRAHAM HATFIELD.

Baker Hendricks and Pheobe Hatfield

HANNAH HENDRICKS.

HANNAH HENDRICKS.

JOHN HENDRICKS.

PHEBE HENDRICKS.

BAKER HENDRICKS.

MARGARET HENDRICKS.

MARGARET HENDRICKS.

ABRAHAM HENDRICKS.

Joseph Ludlum and Anna Hatfield

CORNELIUS LUDLUM, b. 1718; m. Sarah; d. 1799 Essex, New Jesey.

    i.   Cornelius

MATTHIAS LUDLUM, b. 1720; d. 1799 Westfield, Connecticut.

ANN LUDLUM, b. 1725 New Jersey; m. John Searing; d. 12 October 1802.

    i.   William
    ii. Living

John Peter Salnave and
Sarah Hatfield

HANNAH SALNAVE, m. Cornelius Airy; d. 1770.

ELIZABETH SALNAVE, m. Benjamin Smith; d. 1769.

MAGDALEN SALNAVE.

PHOEBE SALNAVE, b. 1723; m. Nathaniel Meeker.

    i.   Gabriel
    ii. Mary Ann
    iii. Uzel

ANN SALNAVE, b. 1724; d. 1828.

PETER SALNAVE, b. 1725 New Jersey; (M1) Abigail Burnett 1751 Elizabethtown, New Jersey; (M2) Abigial Barnes; d. 1757 New Jersey.

   i.   Peter

SARAH SALNAVE, b. 1738; m. Thomas Tobin; d. 1755.

Cornelius Badgley and Mary Hatfield

GEORGE BADGLEY, b. 1726 Elizabethtown, New Jersey; private in Revolutionary War from New Jersey; (M1) Charity Noe; (M2) Esther; d. 25 April 1794 Denville, New Jersey.

George and Charity

   i.   Isaac
  ii. John
 iii. Nancy
 iv. Ichabod
  v. Charity
 vi. Henry
 vii. Anna
viii. Aaron

George and Esther

 ix. Susan

CORNELIUS BADGLEY.

ELIZABETH BADGLEY.

SARAH BADGLEY.

MARY BADGLEY.

RACHEL BADGLEY.

George Badgley Jr. and Rachel Hatfield

NANCY BADGLEY, b. 1718 Elizabethtown, New Jersey.

HANNAH BADGLEY, b. 1720 Elizabethtown, New Jersey.

CORNELIUS BADGLEY, b. 1728 Elizabethtown, New Jersey; m. Elsey Townley; d. 10 June 1794 Elizabethtown, New Jersey.

   i.   Marjorie
  ii. William
 iii. Mary
 iv. Abner
  v. Rachel
 vi. Sarah
 vii. Jane
viii. Edward
 ix. William
  x. Matthias
 xi. James
 xii. Jacob
xiii. Andrew
xiv. Isaac

ELIZABETH BADGLEY, b. 1730 Elizabethtown, New Jersey; (M1) Benjamin Jackson; (M2) John Brown; (M3) Captain Lee.

SARAH BADGLEY, b. 1732 Elizabethtown, New Jersey; (M1)

Robert DeForest; (M2) John Clark; (M3) William Graham; d. 2 November 1793 Elizabethtown, New Jersey.

Sarah and John

    i.   Abigail
    ii.   Sarah
    iii.   John
    iv.   George
    v.   William
    vi.   William

MARY BADGLEY, b. 1739 Elizabethtown, New Jersey; m. James Carmichael.

RACHEL BADGLEY, b. 1741 Elizabethtown, New Jersey.

George Hatfield Jr. and Margaret Winans

ABRAHAM HATFIELD III, b. 1718; d. December 1759.

JOHN HATFIELD, b. about 1722 New Jersey; (M1) Kataherine Supplee 20 November 1736 Philadelphia, Pennsylvania; (M2) Deborah Smith 1744; d. December 1759.

John and Deborah

    i.   Jane
    ii.   Margery
    iii.   John
    iv.   Abel
    v.   Job
    vi.   James

    vii.   Morris
    ix.   Mary
    x.   Deborah
    xi.   Sarah
    xii.   Daniel

SARAH HATFIELD, b. 1724.

DAVID HATFIELD, b. 1723; m. Susanna Clark; d. September 1801.

    i.   Joseph

SAMUEL HATFIELD, b. 1728; d. 2 November 1797.

ELIAS HATFIELD, b. 1729; d. 1789 New Jersey.

JACOB HATFIELD, b. 1730 Elizabeth, New Jersey; m. Mary Lyon; d. 23 August 1774.

    i.   James
    ii.   Jacob
    iii.   Mary
    iv.   Elias
    v.   Abraham

PHOEBE HATFIELD, b. 1731; d. 9 January 1775 Elizabethtown, New Jersey.

WILLIAM HATFIELD, b. 28 December 1736; (M1) Anne Wright; (M2) Sarah Kimball; d. 6 September 1797.

William and Anne

    i.   William

JOSEPH HATFIELD SR., (M1) Elizabeth (Deliz) Vance; (M2) Rachel Smith.

Joseph and Rachel

   i.   Rachel Phariba

JEREMIAH HATFIELD.

GEORGE HATFIELD.

(Descendants of Joseph Sr., Jeremiah and George published in: *Hatfield*, by L.L. Sellars Jr.)

MATTHIAS HATFIELD.

Matthias Hatfield and Hannah Miller

PHOEBE HATFIELD.

HANNAH HATFIELD.

MATTHIAS HATFIELD.

AARON HATFIELD.

MATTHIAS HATFIELD.

ELIZABETH HATFIELD.

JONATHAN HATFIELD.

MOSES HATFIELD.

Joseph Hatfield and Phoebe Clark

MARY ANN HATFIELD

Jacob Hatfield and Mary Lyon

JAMES C. HATFIELD, b. 1753.

Jacob Hatfield and Esther Thomas

ABRAHAM HATFIELD.

MARGARET HATFIELD.

LYDIA HATFIELD.

Peter Decker and Susanne Hatfield

MARIA DECKER.

JOHANNES DECKER.

SUSANNA DECKER.

PETER DECKER.

SARAH DECKER.

MATTHEUS DECKER.

EVA DECKER.

ABRAHAM DECKER.

JACOB DECKER.

Henry Baker and Mary Hatfield

MARY BAKER.

(CHILD) BAKER.

SUSANNA BAKER.

HENRY BAKER.   **MATTHIAS BAKER.**

JACOB BAKER.   **WILLIAM BAKER.**

CORNELIUS BAKER.

GENERATION IV

Aaron Clark and Susanna Winans

WINANS CLARK, b. 12 January 1778 New Jersey; m. Nancy Foreman; d. 7 August 1840 Arkansas.

    i.   Sarah
    ii.   Abraham
    iii.   Abigail
    iv.   Aaron
    v.   Susan
    vi.   Elizabeth
    vii.   Harriet
    viii.   Ann

ELIZABETH CLARK, b. 1780 New Jersey; m. Zadoc Cramer; d. 5 May 1818 Pittsburg, Pennsylvania.

    i.   Susan

HATFIELD CLARK.

JOSIAH CLARK, b. before 1790; (M1) Grace; (M2) Elizabeth McClain; d. 1841.

Josiah and Grace

    i.   Mary

Josiah and Elizabeth

    ii.   Nimrod
    iii.   James
    iv.   Abraham

    v.   Lizzie
    vi.   Harriet

HANNAH CLARK

ABIGAIL CLARK, b. 1805 Pennsylvania; m. William McLean 7 March 1821 Cleveland, Ohio; d. 26 August 1846 Clarksville, Arkansas.

    i.   Leander
    ii.   Serena
    iii.   Antoinette
    iv.   Cecilia

SUSANNAH CLARK, b. 1833.

Thomas Clark and Elizabeth Dixon

JONATHAN CLARK, b. 5 September 1776 Elizabethtown, New Jersey; m. Catherine Jonas 14 September 1800 Maryland; d. 12 December 1849 Maquoketa, Iowa.

    i.   Mary
    ii.   Lucyan
    iii.   Samuel
    iv.   David
    v.   John
    vi.   William
    vii.   David
    viii.   Jonas
    ix.   Elizabeth
    x.   Susannah
    xi.   Alfred

xii.   Catharine
xiii. Lucinda
xiv.   Jonathan

DAVID CLARK, d. Allegany County, Maryland.

ABRAHAM CLARK, b. 1785; m. Lydia Ridgway; d. 17 March 1858.

Clarkson Edgar and Sarah Clark

ELIZA CLARK, b. 28 August 1792; m. John Pruyn Beekman 19 May 1821; d. 17 November 1875.

i.   Catharine
ii.   Anna

Thomas Salter and Abigail Clark

GEORGE WRIGHT SALTER, b. February 1804; d. 17 June 1805.

LOUISA ABBY WRIGHT SALTER, b. 14 March 1805.

Xenophon Jouet and Gertrude Garrison

ABIGAIL JOUET

SARAH JOUET

CAVALIER HAMILTON JOUET, m. Mary Buchanan King.

i.   Xenophon (plus 6 other unknown siblings)

SUSAN JOUET

THOMAS JOUET

ANN JOUET

GERTRUDE JOUET

BEVERLY JOUET

ISAAC JOUET

Jacob Dehart and Sarah Jouet

JOHN DEHART

MARY ROBERSON DEHART

ELIZA DEHART, b. 1800; d. 9 July 1802 Philadelphia, Pennsylvania.

SARAH DEHART, b. 1801.

Cornelius Ludlum and Sarah

CORNELIUS LUDLUM

John Searing and Ann Ludlum

WILLIAM SEARING

LIVING SEARING

Nathaniel Meeker and Phoebe Salnave

GABRIEL MEEKER

MARY ANN MEEKER

UZEL MEEKER

PETER SALNAVE

George Badgley and Charity Noe

ISAAC BADGLEY, b. 1750 Elizabethtown, New Jersey; Revolutionary War Vet; m. Joanna Sweazy 12 April 1777 Elizabethtown, New Jersey.

   i.   Philemon

JOHN BADGLEY, b. 1752 Elizabethtown, New Jersey; m. Charity Force; d. 1793 Caldwell, New Jersey; British Loyalist, John Howard's New York Vol. as Private.

   i.   Sarah
   ii.   Susanna
   iii.   Hannah
   iv.   Mary
   v.   Elizabeth
   vi.   Jinnet
   vii.   Samuel Force
   viii.   Rachel
   ix.   Electa
   x.   Thomas Palmer

NANCY BADGLEY, b. 1754 Elizabethtown, New Jersey; m. John Brown.

   i.   Rachel
   ii.   James Jr.
   iii.   William
   iv.   Sally
   v.   Polly

ICHABOD BADGLEY, b. 1758 Elizabethtown, New Jersey; m. Sarah Hattaway 18 April 1781 Morristown, New Jersey; d. 1803 Phelps, New York.

   i.   Lydia
   ii.   Charity
   iii.   Timothy
   iv.   Demas
   v.   Joanna
   vi.   Thankful
   vii.   John

CHARITY BADGLEY, b. 1760 Elizabethtown, New Jersey; m. Peter Hill Jr. 18 April 1781 Morristown, New Jersey.

   i.   Rachel
   ii.   Daniel
   iii.   Elizabeth
   iv.   Aaron
   v.   Sarah
   vi.   Ichabod
   vii.   Esther
   viii.   Lewis
   ix   Catherine

HENRY BADGLEY, b. 1764 Denville, New Jersey; m. Abigail Howell; d. 13 March 1814 Denville, New Jersey.

   i.   Isaac
   ii.   Nancy
   iii.   Demas
   iv.   Hanna
   v.   Martha
   vi.   Sally

vii. Eliza
viii. Maria
ix. Eunice

ANNA BADGLEY, b. 1767 Denville, New Jersey; m. Captain David Hill; d. 1813.

AARON BADGLEY, b. 10 August 1771 Deanville, New Jersey; m. Joanna Hedges 1791; d. 4 April 1855 LaSalle County, Illinois.

    i. Ruth
    ii. John
    iii. Lucy
    iv. Mary
    v. George
    vi. Sarah
    vii. Lavina
    viii. Anthony
    ix. Joanna
    x. Lucena
    xi. Aaron

George Badgley and Esther

SUSAN BADGLEY, b. 1786 Deanville, New Jersey; d. 1855.

Cornelius Badgley and Elsey Townley

MARJORIE BADGLEY, b. 16 September 1753 Elizabethtown, New Jersey; m. Abner Price.

    i. Isaac
    ii. Edward
    iii. Obadiah
    iv. Cornelius

v. Elsey
vi. Jacob
vii. Abigail

WILLIAM BADGLEY, b. 1755 Elizabethtown, New Jersey.

MARY BADGLEY, b. 1 May 1757 Elizabethtown, New Jersey.

ABNER BADGLEY, b. 1758 Elizabethtown, New Jersey.

    i. Elizabeth
    ii. Jane
    iii. Abigail

RACHEL BADGLEY, b. 28 June 1760 Elizabethtown, New Jersey; m. Thomas Price; d. 17 January 1839.

    i. Caleb
    ii. Jane
    iii. Elias
    iv. Jeremiah
    v. Henrietta
    vi. Mary
    vii. Britton
    viii. Sarah
    ix. Joseph
    x. Joanna
    xi. Phebe
    xii. Abigail
    xiii. Maria
    xiv. James
    xv. Thomas

SARAH BADGLEY, b. 1762 Elizabethtown, New Jersey.

JANE BADGELY, b. 1764 Elizabethtown, New Jersey; m. Quigley; d. 20 July 1809 Kingston, Canada.

    i.   Ogden
    ii. John

EDWARD BADGLEY, b. 1766 Elizabethtown, New Jersey; d. 20 July 1809 Neward, New Jersey.

    i.   Mary
    ii. John

WILLIAM BADGLEY, b. 13 October 1767 Elizabeth-town, New Jersey; m. Rebecca Abbott; d. 11 November 1825 Elizabethtown, New Jersey.

    i.   Abigail
    ii.   Unk.
    iii. Catherine
    iv. Joseph
    v.   Cornelius
    vi. Unk.
    vii. Mary

MATTHIAS BADGELY, b. 1771 Elizabethtown, New Jersey; m. Rachel Abbott; d. 7 June 1851 Ernesttown, Upper Canada.

    i.   Mary
    ii.   Alice
    iii. James
    iv. Joseph
    v.   William
    vi. Henry
    vii. Jane

JAMES BADGLEY, b. 1773 Elizabethtown, New Jersey

JACOB BADGLEY, b. 1775 Elizabethtown, New Jersey.

ANDREW BADGLEY, b. 1777 Elizabethtown, New Jersey; (M1) Esther; (M2) Nancy Daughters; d. 1839 White Oak, Ohio.

Andrew and Esther

    i.   Robert
    ii.   Sarah
    iii. Polly
    iv. Isaac
    v.   Elizabeth
    vi. William
    vii. Jane
    viii. Andrew
    ix. James

Andrew and Nancy

GEORGE JOSEPH

ISAAC BADGLEY, b. 8 April 1780 Elizabethtown, New Jersey; (M1) Eliza; (M2) Anna; d. 24 June 1852 Randolph County, Indiana.

Isaac and Eliza

    i.   Loruhama
    ii.   John
    iii. William

Isaac and Anna

iv.   James

John Clark and Sarah Badgley

SARAH CLARK, b. 1750's Elizabethtown, New Jersey; m. John Van Dyk 18 February 1778 Elizabethtown, New Jersey; d. before 1788 Elizabethtown, New Jersey.

   i.   James
   ii. Ellenor
   iii. Sarah
   iv. Mariah

JOHN CLARK, b. 1757/8 Elizabethtown, New Jersey; m. Amy Hoplins August 1777 North Providence, Rhode Island; d. 27 April 1794 Elizabethtown, New Jersey.

   i.   Stephen
   ii. (child)
   iii. John

ABIGAIL CLARK, b. 30 November 1759 Elizabeth-town, New Jersey; m. Morris Hatfield; d. 19 May 1853 Elizabethtown, New Jersey.

   i.   Mary

GEORGE CLARK, b. 1763 Elizabethtown, New Jersey; d. 1765?

WILLIAM ANDERSON CLARK.

WILLIAM CLARK, b. 1766 Elizabethtown, New Jersey; d. before August 1795.

Blanchard and (female) Hatfield

LEWIS BLANCHARD.

John Hatfield and Deborah Smith

JANE HATFIELD.

MARGERY HATFIELD, b. 1747; m. Jacob Tooker, a Tory; d. August 1831.

   i.   Mary
   ii. Deborah
   iii. Joseph
   iv. Margery
   v.   Sarah

JOHN SMITH HATFIELD, miserable Tory.

ABEL HATFIELD, b. 1752

BR. COL. JOB HATFIELD, b. 2 January 1754; Tory; (M1) Jane Smith; (M2) Jane Van Norden; d. 13 April 1825 Tusket, Nova Scotia.

Job and Jane Smith

   i.   Phebe

Job and Jane Van Norden

   ii. John
   iii. Deborah

iv. Gabriel
v. Pheobe
vi. Magdalen
vii. Jane
viii. Job
ix. Cornelius
x. Margery
xi. Theodosia
xii. Sarah

JAMES HATFIELD, b. 1756; Tory.

MAJ. MORRIS HATFIELD, b. 1759; Patriot.

MARY HATFIELD, b. 1759; m. Gen. Mooers.

DEBORAH HATFIELD, m. Robert Spencer, Patriot.

SARAH HATFIELD, b. 1763; Patriot.

DANIEL HATFIELD, b. 1765,

David Hatfield and Susanna Clark

JOSEPH HATFIELD, b. 19 June 1756 Elizabethtown, New Jersey; m. Anna Rannels; d. 29 December 1815 Lebanon, Ohio.

i. Clark

Jacob Hatfield and Mary Lyon

JAMES HATFIELD, b. 1753.

JACOB LYON HATFIELD, b. 9 December 1757 Elizabeth, New Jersey.

MARY HATFIELD, b. 1761.

ELIAS WINANS HATFIELD, b. 1766.

ABRAHAM MARSH HATFIELD, b. 15 January 1767.

William Hatfield and Anne Wright

WILLIAM HATFIELD, b. 6 January 1759; m. Charity.

i. Adam

Joseph Hatfield (M2) Rachel Smith

RACHEL PHARIBA HATFIELD, m. Isaack Reed; See Remaining Pedigree of Richard Scott Baskas (author)

REMAINING PEDIGREE OF RICHARD SCOTT BASKAS

GENERATION VII

*Isaack Reed and
Rachel Phariba Hatfield*

PHARIBA REED, b. 1810 Scott County, Tennessee; m. James Timothy Cecil; d. 23 December 1881 Helenwood, Tennessee. There are two girls who were kidnapped and never seen again.

i.   Samuel
ii.   Sarah
iii. William R.
iv.   Granville
v.   Riley
vi.   Isaac
vii. Charity
viii. Rebecca
ix.   Catherine
x.   Martin
xi.   Nelson
xii. Pharaba
xiii. Malinda
xiv. Elizabeth
xv.   Phoebe
xvi. Allen
xvii. Nancy

ALLEN REED, b. 1811 Tennessee; d. 1901 Tennessee.

SARAH REED, b. 1812 Tennessee; d. 1901 Tennessee

DELILAH REED, b. 1815 Scott County, Tennessee; m. John Lewallen; d. 24 May 1865 Scott County, Tennessee

ELIZABETH REED, b. 1817 Tennessee; d. 24 May 1865 Tennessee

CAMPBELL COUNTY REED, b. 30 April 1820 Scott County, Tennessee; m. Martha "Patsy" Ann Chitwood; d. 11 July 1886 Scott County, Tennessee.

i.   Rachel
ii.   Rebecca
iii. Sarah "Sallie"
iv.   Martha
v.   Jupiter
vi.   Joel
vii. Sampson
viii. Delilah

ANDREW REED, 10 June 1823 Scott County, Tennessee; m. Zilpha Buttram, 1846 Scott County, Tennessee; Farmer by occupation; Civil War Vet; d. 5 September 1904 Ozark County, Missouri; buried Hawkins Ridge, Bakersville; Zilpha, b. 1826 Morgan Co, Tennessee, d. 1865 Scott County, Tennessee.

i.   Allen
ii.   Rebecca
iii. Clerinda
iv.   John
v.   Granville

REBECCA REED, b. 1825 Scott County, Tennessee; d. 5 September 1904 Tennessee

SAMPSON REED, b. 1 October 1827 Scott County, Tennessee; (M1) Sarah McDonald; (M2) Eliza Jane Thompson; (M3) Sarah Phillips; d. 27 February 1890

ISAAC REED, b. 30 January 1830 Scott County, Tennessee; m. Emily

JOHN REED, b. 9 October 1832; m. Pernetta Bowling; d. 18 October 1879

MELINDA EMILY REED, b. 9 February 1834 Tennessee; m. Sterling McDonald; d. 17 March 1907 Texas

ELIZA JANE REED, b. 1837 Tennessee; m. Ezekiel Newport; d. 17 March 1907 Tennessee

GENERATION VIII

Phariba Reed and James Cecil

SAMUEL CECIL

SARAH CECIL

WILLIAM R. CECIL

GRANVILLE CECIL

RILEY CECIL

ISAAC CECIL

CHARITY CECIL

REBECCA CECIL

CATHERINE CECIL

MARTIN CECIL

NELSON CECIL

PHARABA CECIL

MALINDA CECIL

ELIZABETH CECIL

PHOEBE CECIL

ALLEN CECIL

NANCY CECIL

*Campbell Reed and
Martha Chitwood*

RACHEL REED, b. 1841; m. K. David Murphy 17 November 1865.

REBECCA REED, b. 1843; m. James G. Chitwood 16 February 1865.

SARAH "SALLIE" REED, b. 1844; m. Joseph Terry Smith 26 March 1869; d. 1918.

    i.   Nancy
    ii.   Ezra

iii. Rebecca
iv. John
v. William
vi. Zora
vii. Cornell
viii. Rachel

MARTHA ANN REED, b. 1847; m.
Jonathan Phillips 4 February 1869

JUPITER REED, b. 1850.

JOEL C. REED, b. 1 September 1850;
d. 1 November 1933.

SAMPSON REED, b. 15 January 1853
Tennessee; d. 18 May 1941 Tennessee.

DELILAH REED, b. 13 January 1855;
m. W. F. Thomas 15 March 1877; d.
24 February 1925.

Andrew Reed and Zilpha Buttram

ALLEN REED, b. 1846 Scott County,
Tennessee

REBECCA REED, 1849 Scott County,
Tennessee

CLERINDA REED, b. 1851 Scott
County, Tennessee

JOHN REED, 1855 Scott County,
Tennessee

GRANVILLE REED, b. 8 June 1859
Scott County, Tennessee; m. Nicey
Caroline Knight, 19 April 1887

Bakersfield, Missouri; d. 27 June
1940 Bayou, Arkansas; Nicey, b.
7 December 1857 Tennessee (Full
Cherokee), d. 1 April 1928 Bayou,
Arkansas both buried Flutys Chapel
Cemetery, Gamaliel.

i.   Cora Belle
ii.   Henry A.
iii. Andrew J.
iv.   Lonnie
v.   Herman
vi.   Thurman
vii. Caroline
viii. infant

(Pedigree of RSB)

GENERATION IX

Sarah Reed and Joseph Smith

NANCY SMITH

EZRA SMITH

Rebecca Smith

John Smith

William Campbell Smith

Zora Bell Smith, m. Sackrider

Cornell Smith

Rachel Cordenia Smith, b. 11 April 1873; m. Haywood Pemberton.

Granville Reed and Caroline Knight

Infant Reed

Henry A. Reed, b. February 1881 Ozark County, Missouri.

Cora Belle Reed, b. 1882 Baxter County, Arkansas; (M1) Thomas Bradee Eaiston; (M2) Joe Henson 1913; Joe was known to be a very hard working man. He could work from sun up to sun down in the cotton patch and not even stop for lunch. He could not read or write; d. 1942 Tupelo, Arkansas; Joe died 20 August 1950/9 Tuttle, Oklahoma.

Cora and Thomas

i.   Lillie Dale

Cora and Joe

ii.   Stella Della
iii. Ella

iv.   Newton Carl
v.   Lizzie/Lee/Leon
vi.   Edith
vii. Kenneth
viii. Roy
ix.   Claude
x.   Cleo "Curly" Hubert

Andrew J. Reed, b. March 1883 Baxter County, Arkansas.

Lonnie Reed, b. March 1888 Baxter County, Arkansas.

Herman Reed, b. September 1891 Baxter County, Arkansas.

Pencie Reed, b. May 1898 Baxter County, Arkansas.

Thruman Reed, b. 22 March 1896 Gamaliel, Arkansas; Army, WW I, Company K, 45th Infantry in 11 October 1917; discharged 11 January 1919; m. Emma Caroline Foster, b. 14 February 1900, d. 24 March 1981 Mountain Home, Arkansas, buried Fluty Cemetery, Gamaliel; d. 4 March 1981 Mountain Home, Arkansas.

i.   Herbert
ii.   Elsie
iii. Virgie
iv.   Anna
v.   Ruby
vi.   Ongil
vii. Margie
viii. Edna

    ix.   Elva
    x.   LaVern
    xi.   David

GENERATION X

Cora Reed and Thomas Eaiston

LILLIE DALE EAISTON, b. 15 January 1903 Tupelo, Arkansas; m. William Umphrey Campbell 16 February 1923 Tupelo, Arkansas; d. 1964 Poplar Bluff, Missouri.

    i.   Flay
    ii.   Clettea
    iii. Clyde

Cora Reed and Joe Henson

STELLA DELLA HENSON, b. 4 December 1905 Mountain Home, Arkansas. There's not much that I have been able to find on her, from her birth all the way to where she lived in Missouri. Her daughter, Donna, mentioned that Grandma would tell them ghost stories and play with them by sneaking around and scaring them; (M1) Houston Canard (b. 1901 Arkansas) about 1922. They lived in Augusta, Woodruff County, Arkansas in 1930 with their daughter, Lois, as they were renting a farm there. The earliest that any of Grandma's children can remember of her is that Donna told me that Grandma had taken their daughters to Tupelo to buy them a red dress, as they were going to take a train to New Port, which is 19 miles from Tupelo. Then all of a sudden, they saw this man that would eventually become Betty's father; (M2) Arthur Samuel Karnes. Nothing is known of this marriage other than he became or was a drunk and was abusive; (M3) Robert F. North on 26 June 1954 in Kansas City, Missouri but no children. It seemed that Betty and Robert didn't get along and so Grandma had her moved in with a family that Grandma knew in Leavenworth who would care for her as she was still in school. Grandma used to work for Independence Laundry at the time. Not long after, she divorced Robert, but kept his surname. It seems that soon after, she would move to Merced, California sometime in the 1960's to be with one of her daughters who needed her support for medical reasons. Grandma would live by herself in her own trailer in Merced next to her daughter. She would live here for years until she and her daughter and son-in-law would move and she would live in La Sierra Convalescent Home and would pass away on 22 December 1992. She was buried in Winton Cemetery in Winton.

(Pedigree of RSB)

Stella and Houston

i. Lois
ii. Clara
iii. Donna
iv. JoAnn
v. Wilma

Stella and Arthur

vi. Betty

ELLA MAE HENSON, b. 1907 Baxter County, Arkansas.

NEWTON CARL HENSON, b. 4 April 1910 Gamaliel, Arkansas; d. 17 February 1987 Tuttle, Oklahoma; m. Audrie Minnie Hood, 30 September 1927 Mayes County, Oklahoma; he farmed most of his life. He retired from the Oklahoma highway department working as a flagman on the road crew. He loved to fish and hunt. He always carried enough fishing poles in the trunk of his old car to all of his kids could go fishing. Of course his kids spent most of their time trying to catch enough grasshoppers for bait when they ran out of worms. He could always take time to go "mushroom huntin'". He used to go Polksalad hunting a lot but everybody liked mushin' better than the greens. Audrey was a housewife. She loved to go to church and to sing even though she couldn't a tune or even keep time. She always walked to town to do her "tradin'". She had a stroke and was wheelchair bound for the last ten years or so of her life. Had 5 children.

i. Nellie Mae, d. age 5 years old of Diphtheria; buried Tuttle Cemetery

LIZZIE/LEE/LEON HENSON, b. 16 February 1911 Gamaliel, Arkansas; d. 1985 Tuttle, Oklahoma.

EDITH HENSON, b. 4 April 1914 Gamaliel, Arkansas; m. Homer Hoover.

i. Bill

KENNETH HENSON, b. 1917 Missouri; m. Martha; d. Clarkston, Missouri.

ROY HENSON, b. 16 December 1919 Gamaliel, Arkansas; m. Lois; d. 6 March 1981 Van Buren, Arkansas.

Claude Henson, m. Wanda McKinney; d. Austin, Texas.

Cleo "Curly" Hubert Henson, b. 1928 Tuttle, Oklahoma.

*Thruman Reed and
Emma Caroline Foster*

Herbert Ray Reed, b. 12 March 1920 Gamaliel, Arkansas; m. Alberta Mae Waters 6 December 1947; Alberta d. February 1994; d. 27 January 2003; both buried Chapel Hill Cemetery, Kansas City, Kansas.

Elsie L. Reed, b. 17 February 1922 Gamaliel, Arkansas.

Virgie Reed, b. 17 November 1924 Gamaliel, Arkansas.

Anna Lee Reed, b. 14 June 1927 Gamaliel, Arkansas.

Ruby M. Reed, b. 13 February 1929 Gamaliel, Arkansas.

Orgil Reed, b. 22 February 1931 Gamaliel, Arkansas.

Margie Reed, b. 24 October 1932 Gamaliel, Arkansas; (M1) Paul Roper 23 September 1950 Viola, Arkansas; (M2) Charles Winchester 14 February 1984; d. 18 November 1999 Gamaliel, Arkansas; buried Flora Cemetery near Viola, Arkansas.

Edna Reed, b. 24 June 1935 Gamaliel, Arkansas.

Elva Reed, b. 26 November 1936 Gamaliel, Arkansas.

LaVern Reed, b. 28 November 1939 Gamaliel, Arkansas.

David Reed, b. 6 January 1944 Gamaliel, Arkansas.

Generation XI

*Lillie Eaiston and
William Campbell*

Flay Campbell, b. 22 May 1924 Tupelo, Arkansas; (M1) Viola Mae Teague 9 July 1948 Tulare, California; (M2) Sarah (Sally) Carter; d. 27 June 1989 Memphis, Tennessee.

Flay and Viola

i.   Patsy
ii. Lloyd
iii. Donna

Stella Henson and Houston Canard

Lois Virginia Canard, b. 1926 Arkansas; (M1?); (M2) Frank Chaves.

Lois and (M1?)

i.   Jimmy Dean
ii. Virginia Lou

iii. Ronny Allen
iv. Peggy Ann

Lois and Frank Chaves

v. Linda

CLARA ODELL CANARD, m. Robert Dorsey

i. Sharon
ii. David
iii. Rickey

DONNA BELL CANARD, (M1?); (M2) Bill Willoughby; has 2 girls.

JOANN CANARD, m. Holzbar; has 2 boys.

WILMA JEAN CANARD, m. Sanders; has 8 children.

Stella Henson and Arthur Karns

BETTY EMMA KARNES, b. 12 December 1946 Kansas City, Missouri; As a child she never really knew her immediate family as she was given to another family. By the time she was in school, her older sisters were basically already married and had moved out on their own. Her mother had then divorced her father and had then been remarried, to Robert North. She attended North Broadway School, '58-'61, and North Rock Creek; attended Leavenworth Jr. High finishing only 10th grade. She later met and married my father, James Anthony Baskas, of Leavenworth, Kansas. In early 1970's they both divorced and she would marry an army veteran from the fort. They would move to Fort Sam Houston, Texas where she would later join the Army. Before being sent on one of her tours in Korea, she married William H. Brown. After she served in Korea, she adopted a boy from there and brought him back. She would soon separate from the Army and work as a software applications instructor until her retirement from the fort.

(Pedigree of RSB)

Betty and James

i. Richard
ii. James

Betty and William

iii. Jerrad "J.B." Harrison

Homer Hoover and Edith Henson

BILL HOOVER, b. 21 February 1936 Tuttle, Oklahoma; m. Bonnie Marie Newman 20 August 1960 Oklahoma City, Oklahoma; d. 13 January 2003 Chickasha.

i.   Michael
ii. Michelle

GENERATION XII

Betty Karnes and James Baskas

RICHARD SCOTT BASKAS, b. 8 April 1965 Merced, California; attended schools in Clinton, Maryland where he and his brother were brought up by another family; Currently holds A.A., General Studies, Charles County Community College, LaPlata, Maryland, 1987; B.S., Biology, Salisbury State University, Salisbury, Maryland, 1990; U.S.A.F. (honorable), 8 April 1992-30 April 2004, Firefighter, Driver, Crew Chief, Station Captain and 911 Dispatcher; A.A.S., Fire Science, Community College of the A.F., 1986; Bases stationed: Langley AFB, Virginia; Soto Cano AB, Honduras; MacDill AFB, Florida; Al Dhafra AB, United Arab Emirates (UAE); Columbia, South America and Eskan Village, Saudi Arabia; Medals and Awards include: Air Force Achievement Medal; Joint Meritorious Unit Award; Outstanding Unit Award; Organization Excellence Award; Good Conduct Medal; National Defense Service Medal; Armed Forces Expeditionary Medal; Southwest Asia Campaign; Humanitarian Service Medal; Overseas Short Tour; Longevity Service Award; NCO Professional Military Education Graduate; Air Force Training; Currently works as one of 911 Dispatchers for MacDill AFB, Florida; Currently enrolled in Master of Arts in Teaching (M.A.T.) program, Science Education, University of South Florida, Tampa, Florida.

Authored: *My Family History: Pioneers of Custer County, Montana and Leavenworth, Kansas: Descendants of Kanelly, Barry, Roache, Pike, Baskas and McMahon.* Xlibris Pub. Co., Philadelphia, PA: 2007.

(Pedigree of RSB)

[Mendenhall Glacier, Juneau, Alaska, July, 2007; picture by David J. Price, Anchorage, Alaska]

JAMES ALLEN BASKAS, b. 8 May 1967 Leavenworth, Kansas; attended schools in Clinton, Maryland; worked in air conditioning and refrigeration trade; d. 23 April 2003 Deltona, Florida; buried Mt. Calvary Cemetery, Lansing, Kansas.

B.S., Biology; m. Christine Rios 12 May 2003 San Antonio, Texas; Christina, B.S., Nursing, University of the Incarnate Word, 10 May 2003, San Antonio.

(Pedigree of RSB)

(Pedigree of RSB)

Betty Karnes and William Brown

JERRAD "J.B." HARRISON BROWN, b. 1 January 1977 Taesu, South Korea;

Jacob Melyn

Jacob was born about 1639 and baptized on 17 April 1640 by Dr. Somerus, which was witnessed by Nelletje Dircx in Nieuwe Kerk, Amsterdam. He came to New Netherland with his parents on *The Oak Tree* in 1641. After the Indian massacre in September 1655 where he "was much wounded, but recovered, not without great difficulty." [98]

Mr. Melyn rebuked, 4 October 1656:

A complainte was made by some that ye Duchmen lately admitted doe sell things excessive deare, and instanc was given in some particulers, but a knott of buttons was now showed in ye meeting, small silke buttons at 18d a dosson, wch was looked at as a most exceeding dear price, like wise that the mault house is not improued, as Mr. Melyen promised it should, to supply ye Town,e also that they doe not attend ye publique meetings on ye Lords day so duely as they should: aboute wch things the Court, wch Mr. Davenport, the decons & Townsmen, were desired to meete this after-nooe and speake wth ym, that so what is offensive me be removed.

He went to New Haven with his parents where they took the formal Oath of Fidelity in 1657. He received a large grant of land and became one of the active leaders in Elizabethtown as he became a Burgess. He also was to become a partner in the whaling business. He sold his home lot of four acres, with the buildings, which had been erected to his brother-in-law, John Winans, before he moved to New York, then to Boston, Jacob occasionally visited New Amsterdam during the next 5-6 years, but maintained his residence in New Haven. He, his brother, Isaac, and their father sailed from New England to Holland in 1658 and returned to New Netherland on De Liefde (The Love) in 5 March 1660. [99]

Hanky Panky, New Haven 1660 Style, 1 May 1660:

Jacob Murline & Sarah Tuttle being called appeared, concerning whom the governor declared that the businesse for wch they were warned to the Court he had heard in private at this house, wch he related to stand thus: on the day yt John Potter was married, Sarah Tuttle went ot Mrs. Murlines for some threed; Mrs. Murline bid her goe to her daughters in the other roome, where they fell into speech of John Potter & his wife, that they wer both lame, upon wch Sarah Tuttle said that she wondered what they would doe at night, whereupon Jacob came in & tooke up her gloves to wch he answere, he would doe so, if she would give him a kisse, upon wch they sate downe together, his arme beig about her, & her arme upon his shoulder or about his necke, & he kissed her & shee him, or they kissed one another, continuing in this posture about half an houre, as Mariah & Susan testified, wch Mariah now in Court affirmed to be so. Mrs. Murline now in Court said that she head her say, she wondered what they would doe at night, & she replied they must sleep, but there was company with her in ye roome, & she was in a strait; but it is matter os sorrow & shame to her. Jacob was asked what he had to say to these things theings; to wch he answered yt he was in the other roome, & when he heard Sarah speake those words he went in, hwere shee having let fall her gloves, he tooke them up & she asked him for them; hee told her he would if shee would kisse him, wch she did; further said that he tooke her by ye hand & they both sate downe upon a chest, but whether his arme were about her, & her arme upon his shoulder or about his neck, he knows not, for he never thought of it since, till Mr. Rraymond told him of it at ye Mannatoes; for wch he was blamed & told yt it appears that he hath not layd it to heart as he ought. But Sarah Tuttle replyed that shee did not kiss him; Mr. Tuttle said yt Mariah hath denyed it, & he doth not looke upon her a competent witnesse. Tho. Tuttle in Court affirmed that he asked Mariah if his sister kist Jacob, and she said, noe. Moses mansfeild testified that he told Jacob that he heard yt Sarah kissed him, but he denyed it; but Jacob grantoed not what Moses testified. Mr. Tuttle pleaded that Jacob had endeavourved to steale away his daughter affections; but Sarah being asked if Jacob had inveigled her, she said, no; Tho. Tuttle said that he came to their house tow or three times before he went to Hollad, & they tow were together, &

to what end he came he knows not, unless it were to inveigle her, &
their mother warned Sarah not to keep company with him; & to the
same purpose spake Jonath. Tuttle; but Jacob denyed that he came
to their house with any such intendmt, nor did it appeare so to the
Court. The Governor told Sarrah that her miscarriage is the greatest
that a virgin should be so bold, in the presence of others, to carry it
as she had done, & to speake such corrupt words, most of the things
charged being acknowledged by her self, though that about kissing
him is denyed, yet the thing is proved. Sarah professed that she was
sorry that she had carried it so foolishly & sinfully, wch she sees to
be hatefull; she hoped God would help her to carry it better for time
to come. The governor also told Jacob that his carriage hath beene
very evill and sinfull, so th carry towards her; & to make such a
light matter of it as not to think of it (as he had exprest) doth greatly
aggravate; & for Mariah who was a married woman to suffer her
brother & a mans ddaughter to sitt almost half an houre in such a
way as they have related is a very great evill; shee was told that she
should have shewed her indignation against & have told her mother
that she might have beene shut out of doores. Mrs. Murline was told
that she heareing such words should bot have suffered it. Mr. Tuttle
& MR. Murline being sked if they had any more to say, the said, no;
whereupon ye Court declared that we have heard in the publique
ministry that it is a thing to be lamented that youne peole should have
their meetings, to the corrupting of themselues & one another; as for
Sarah Tuttle, her miscarriages are very great, that she should utter
so corrupt a speech as she did concerning ye persons to be married,
& that she should carry it in such an immodest, uncivell, wanton,
lascivious manner, as hath been proved; & for Jacob, his carriage hath
been very corrupt & sinfull, such as brings reproach upon the family
& place; the sentence therefore concerning them was, that they shall
pay either of them as a fine 20 s to the Treasurer.

After a lengthy hearing in Court, Jacob and Sarah Tuttle were each fined
20 schillings. The story marks the conflict between the Puritan and the
Flemish ways of life, as does also a somewhat similar occurrence in the life
of Jacob's younger brother, Isaac. Both fell afoul of the noted Blue Laws of
New Haven. On 7 January 1661-2, he was sued at New Haven in regard to
a partnership agreement of 29 July 1661 with Nathaniel Street, concerning
the vessel Adventure and a judgment for L15 was rendered against him: [100]

7 October 1662, Jacob Melyn in trouble again!

*Jacob Moloine (was called) with his wife to anser for their goeing together in such a sinful way of fornication as they had done before marriage: they was wished seriously to consider of their sin & how they had exposed themselves to the just judgement of god upon them & could not expect a blessing upon them in yt relation wherein they now was. Jacob Answereed yet for ye fact he had nothing to ssay to excuse himselfe, but he did confesse yt their case thereby was miserable, & that god had made him sensible of it, & he hoped that he would helpe him to be soe more & more; he desired to stand to the mercy of god and of the Court in this business; The Court told him yt he had tempted his wife to this sin & yt his sin was greatly aggrauated in his abusing of scripture to draw her to sin, objecting against yt speech of Christ to the woman taken in adultery John 8. sin no more; which his wife alleged but he said shee was a married woman but it was noe sin in single persons as appears in her examination taken before the Gouernor August 8ᵗʰ (62) which [7] was now read & shee owned & he alsoe, though he said he could not remember some part of it. The Court endeauouring furher to convince them both of their sin both him in tempting her & shee alsoe in her too ready compliance with him proceeded to sentence; & first of him The Court declared that they had Considered of his great sin in this, & how he had formerly beene fined ** in this Court for such kind of wayes in a lesser degree & yet he had not taken warneing thereby but proceeded now to higher acts of filthiness; Therefore sentenced him to be corporally punished by whipping; And for his wife that shee pay a fine of foure pounds to ye Publique.*

At a court held at Newhauen Octob: 7ᵗʰ

Mr. Moline & his wife appeared before ye Court to intreate of them yt they would Consider ye stae of their sonne in reference to ye former sentence, if inflicted, & declared as followeth (as was interprted by Mr. goodenhouse) That he understands that his sonne is sentenced to be coporally punished for his fowle fact committed & he justifies the Court therein: yet seeing his sonne ws to trade with ye dutch as well as the English for the maintenance of his family: Now to be corporally punished wwas such an infamy among yt nation yt they looked upon such noe better then a dog & not fit for commerce wth them &soe his sonne would be undone thereby. Mrs. Moline alsoe justifying the Court desiredwith

much affectioni yt they would free her sonne from thi9s punishment
& she should count it a grat favor & be answerably Thankefull for it.
Mr. Rutherford alsoe declared to ye Court that is was soe amonge ye
dutch as was declared by Mr. Moline; Upon this ye Court declared.
That they had Considered of what hath neene saide by them & of wt
tey haue desired in ye behalfe of their sonne & doe judge the sentence to
be righteoud; yet Considering how destructive it wilbe to your sonne as
is testified they doe passé it by & order your sonne to pay a fine of five
pounds to the Publique. Mr. Moline expressing his thankefulness to ye
Court promised to see both the fines payd to ye Treasurer.

He married Hannah Hubbard in 1662. She was mentioned in her father's will of 23 May 1682. On 7 October 1662, Jacob was sentenced by the New Haven Court "to be corporally punished by whipping" and his wife was ordered to pay a fine of L4 "for their goeing together in such s sinful way***as they had done before marriage." The next day, Jacob's parents appeared in Court and begged that Jacob be let off from the corporal punishment, as it would ruin his trade with the Dutch, since he would be looked upon by them as "noe better than a doe & not fit for commerce with them." Among the Dutch, whipping was a punishment inflicted on a white man for only the most flagrant offenses. "Mr. Rutherford also declared to the Court that it was soe among the Dutch as was declared my Mr. Moline," and the Court was a result of these pleas changed the sentence to a fine of L5. The testimony of Cornelius Melyn and his wife was given in Dutch and interpreted for the Court by Samuel van Godenhuysen, or Goodenhouse.

Elizabethtown, New Jersey

Jacob, Matthis Hatfield, Humphrey Spinning and John Winans were among those of New Haven who were the original Associates who founded Elizabeth Town, New Jersey when they took the Oath of Allegiance and Fidelity "beginning the 19th February 1665/6." He received a large grant of land here and became one of the active leaders in the community. He was Burgess in 1668 and in 1673 was a delegate to negotiate with the authorities for the submission of the Town to the Dutch.

Pronouncement by Gov.; Nickolls to Jacob Melyn, June ye 4th 1668:

Upon the Petition & Request of Mr. Jacob Melyen That his Fathers
interest may be taken into consideration, upon ye settlement of Staten

Island, The governor ordered it to be Entered upon Record that Care should then be had of hin, so farr, as that he shall be allotted a Convenient proportion of Land upon ye said Island, In lieu of what was reserved by his Father, & promised him by ye West India Company.

Extracted out of ye Records in y Office at Fort James in New Yorke. Matthias Nicholls, Secry Endorced: A Copy of a Record of our Interest upon Staten Island ordered by govr Richard Nickills, being ye first English Goverr.

He was a partner in the whaling company in 1669 where he was elected a Schepen (Alderman) on 24 August 1673 and a Militia Captain on 14 September 1673.

Jacob Melyn petitioins Gov. Colve, 1674

To the Hon. Very Respectable Lord Anthony Colve, Governor General and the Lords High Councillors of New Netherland.

Makes known with respectful humility Jacob Melyen, that his deceased father has been proprietor of the Staten Island and has inhabited and possessed the same for many years, until he was surprised by a general war with the savages, many of his children and farmers murdered, their houses and goods burned and destroyed, on account of which great damage and ruin, and also owing to the temporary danger of the savages, he was forced to suffer the said island during some time to remain uninhabited. Some little time afterward he went to Amsterdam and their entered with the Hon. Heeren of the West India company into a contract, concerning the Patroonship and jurisdiction of the said Island, provided he retained to himself, his heirs and successors all his lands, according to the letter of the said contract, of which right your Honrs' petitioner's deceased father and his heirs have been deprived, partley owing to lack of means, sickness and death of your Honrs' petitioner's deceased father, partly owing to the scattered residences, smallness of means and immaturity of years and understanding of his heris, and also partly owing to various changes of government. However your Honors' petitioner having made known his right to the aforesaid, to the first English governor Colonel Nicholls, the latter, before his departure, consented—and had registered by his secretary in the minute book—that a considerable tract of land should be surveyed for the heirs of said Melyen. The last acting governor, Lovles (Lovelace) also several times promised Your Honors' petitioner to permit him to retain and enjoy the same. And about 8 or 10 days before his departure for Hartfort he promised with many words that if God favored him he would have measured for and confirmed to Your Honors' petitioner and friends a parcel of land, situated between two branches of the Millriver, as also [p. 133] the point to the West of the mill, stretching towards to Schoetters Island, which point of land he, Governor Lovles, said he had intended to grant to his brother Thomas Loveles, but desiring to make a reality our long deferred hope, he would qccommodate him [his brother] elsewhere. And whereas I now understand of Thomas Lovles, that he petitions You, Hon. Very Respectable, to t be granted land there, and thus absolutely to deprive my aged mother and her children of all hope ever to receive anything any more of our father's inheritance, the island having been almost entirely apportioned to various individuals.

In consideration of the great expenses and miseries suffered and experienced on the island, therefore I find it my duty, in behalf of myself, wife and children, as well as my brothers and sisters and their children. To pray You Hon. Very resp., very seriously and humbly that you be pleased to deny him Thomas Lovles his desire to obtain any land there, but that you Hon. Very Resp. be pleased to confirm the petitioner and friends in their right, that being delivered through your Hon. Very Resp.'s authority from the English nation, they may again live together in our calling, under our natural Authorities. In expectation of Your Hon. Very Resp's favorable answer, remain Your Hon. Very Rep's subject and servant.

Jacob Melyen
New Orange 1674, April 12/23/06
In the margin of the above petition was written in Dutch:
Fort Wm hendr, Apr. 18, 1674.
The petitioners within fourteen days from date must produce whatever claim they have on any land on Staten Island, or at leas on the land granted to Thomas Lovelace. Dates as above. [p. 134]

By order of the Hon. Heer Governor General and Councillors of New Netherland. N. Bayard, Secretary.

Endorsed in English:
A petition to the Dutch govr Anthony Colve and his Conxill:
Nickols Bayard, Sekretary.
In New Orange 1674: Apr 12/23/06

Grant to Jacob Melyn by Gov. Colve, 12 Oct 1674

Extract from the Register of the Minutes of the Hon. Ld Governor General and Councillors of New Netherland, held in Fort Willem Hendrick, on October 12, 1674

Received and read the petition of the children and heirs of the deceased Cornelius Melyn, assisted by the guardians of the absent heirs of the said estate, and besides the same delivering—in accordance with the order of 18 April last—the documents in proof of their right to Staten island; requesting that, in consideration of the same, they may be shown and granted in ownership a parcel of woodland situated on Staten Island between the two branches of the mill creek, with the point to the West of the said Mill, stretching beyond Schutter's Island to a certain fresh river, running into the country with the valleys bounding on the same; calculating the same to be about a farm for each child; offering at the same time to renounce any further claims thay may have had on the said land; which petition having [p. 135] been taken into consideration the Lord Governor & Councillors (after having examined the produced documents) render the following decision. The petitioners are granted for each child of the deceased Cornelius Melyn, on the said land, a farm of thirty morgen [about 60 acres] amounting for the five children together to one hundred and fifty morgens, provided none of the said lands, prior to this date have been granted [to others] and that thay shall be cultivated by the petitioners as per the orders of the government; In regard to the petitioners further request concerning said parcels of land, they are permitted to have the same measured by the sworn surveyor and further disposition shall be made after receipt of his report.

Agrees with the said register,
N. Bayard, Secretary.

Endorsed in English: A Grant of ye Dutch Govorr Anthy Culve. In answer to ye Petition of Jacob Melyen whereby he grants 5 Farms with Medows sutable & commonages for ye same.

New York

After the fall of Stuyvesant and the capitulation to the English in 1664, Jacob returned to New York and resided there for a number of years. In 1674 and 1677, it would seem that this family made trips to New York as these were baptismal dates of their children. On 9 March 1676/7 he sold some land in Elizabethtown to Nicholas Carter and on 8 February 1677/8 he sold his home lot of four acres, with the building which had been erected on it, to his brother-in-law, John Winans. On 3 February 1674, he purchased a house from Evert Duyckinck and some ground in New York City on the north side of Mill Street (now South William Street). He lived here for many years until he moved to Boston. On 27 May 1684, when his mother died, he received a conveyance of the property through his mother's estate. He didn't remain permanent in New York but was in business as a leather dresser in Boston. This house was on Slyck Steegh, about three city lots. It didn't seem to have been profitable, as on 29 April 1697, he sent a long letter from Boston to Abraham Schellinger (his nephew, son of his sister, Cornelia, wife of Jacob Schellinger) of Easthampton, Long Island, authorizing him to dispose of this property on Mill Street, "and if no sayle can be obtained, nor perso be to be gott to live in't on any acct., then to naile u doors and windows with roff boards, and secure the glass." The property was finally purchased on 28 May 1697 by Dr. Johannes Kerfbyl, the deed being signed by Abraham Schellinger as Attorney for Jacob Melyn.

On 4 December 1682, Jacob went into an agreement with Frederick Phillipse about a voyage to be made to a Spanish wreck on the Bahama Island. On 17 December 1683, Jacob was mentioned as an Assessor for the Dock Ward. On 27 May 1684, he received a conveyance of the property through his mother's estate after she had passed. On 30 June, Richard Pattishall and Joseph Belknap, Junior, became surety to the Town of Boston, for Jacob and his family.

Jacob was evidently a member of a party that supported Jacob Leister, or at least a strong sympathizer (these letters are in New York Colonial Manuscripts). Jacob was an important factor as he was one of the 30 persons named in a law of the Colony of New York, passed on 16 May 1691 as being accepted from the general pardon to those who "had been active in the late disorders." By a subsequent act, passed on 16 May 1699, these 30 were also pardoned.

On 27 July 1693, he was appointed guardian of his nephew Riderus Melyn. On 26 May 1697, he, his wife, and "Samuel Melyn, eldest son and heir at law to the said Jacob Melyn" sold the plot land 19 ½ feet square, situated on southeast corner of present Broad and Stone Streets, portion of what his father had owned, for 360 pounds to William Bickley, a city merchant, who had previously resided in it for some time as a tenant. This small plot of ground has retained its dimensions through nearly two centuries and a half. It is today occupied by a small and somewhat dingy building with some rusty iron fire escapes. [101]

Jacob Melyn's petition, 30 Nov 1698/99

[p. 136] To his Excey Richard Earl of Bellomont, Capt. General & Governor in Chief of his Majties Provinces of the Massachusetts bay, New York, &c and of the Territories theron depending and Vice Admiral of the same.

The humble Petition of Jacob Melyen, most humbly sheweth

That yor Petitioners Father Cornelius Melyen by virtue of a Grant form the West India Company of Holland bearing date the Third of July 1640; was Governr & Proprietr of Staten Island ini the Province of new York & was confirmed in the Governmt and Propriety thereof by Governr Kieft by a Patent bearing date the 19th of June 1642 and was in the quiet Possessioin & Enjoyment of the Governmt and Soyle of the sd Island as his rightfull inheritance, until he with his people [were] driven from thence by the Indians I the year 1643; and he was afte that resettled thereon with diverse families, his servants, until another quarrel was made at New-Amsterdam (now New York) with the Indians, Anno 1655 & were then cutt off upon Staten Island, having about twenty psons slain, who were of sd Melyen's Childrren, nephews, Servants & Tenants. The Town consisting of [p. 137] about forty houses, which were bunt, & the Goods made plunder off, & yor petitioners sd father & mother & two sons with all those that survived were taken into a barbarous Captivity by the heathen; Yor Excellcy's Petitir was one of the Sons who was much wounded, but recovered not without great difficulty. That his sd Father Cornelius Melyen upon some considerations did afterwards, vzt June 13, 1659, Resign his Right og governmt back to the sad. West India Coompany of Holland upon sundry conditions, which were not all by then observed; But he never alienated or sold his Right to the Lands of the sd. Island or any part of

*his Estate there; but expressly reserved the same to himself And his heirs
&c for ever as may appear by the sd agreement between the sd. West
India Company & his sd Father, bearing date the 13ᵗʰ Day of June
1659, and that upon the Delivery of the Governt of New York to the
English, One of the Articles of Agreement between the English & Dutch
Commissioners expressly confirms unto all the Dutch Inhabitants, that
continued there their freedome as Denizens and the Enjoyment of their
Estates as before; Yet he the sd Jacob Melyen hath been ever since by
fraud & Injustice denied and hindred from the Enjoyment of his sd.
Father's Inheritance he being the Rightfull heir, & this notwithstanding
he hath made applicant ot ev'ry Governr that hat been sent thither by
the Kings of England, by which means he hath suffered much Damaged;
All which will pplainly appear to be true by the records of New York,
Copies of which have hitherto been denied the Supplicant.*

*Yor Petitior therefore being well assured of yor Exdellcys great regard
to Impartial Justice most humbly Prays that Yor Excellcy will tatke his
case into Yor serious Consideran and permit him to take out of the
Records copies of such Instruments & Papers as are necessary to prove
ye Truth of what he hath before sett forth in order to Yor Lordship's
more full Satisfacn that Yor Petitir hath a Right to the Soyle [p. 138]
of the sd island & that he may be better enable to possess himself of
the same.*

And Yor Petitir as in duty bound will ever pray etc.
*Endorced: Jacob Melyen's Peitition to his Excellcy Richard Earl of
Bellomont etc.*
Boston, Novembr 30ᵗʰ 1698 [or 99] A copy

Boston, Massachusetts

He moved to Boston where he became a leather dresser and merchant,
like his late father. He became very active as a citizen as he was at times a
Tithing Man, Constable, Clerk of the Market and Surveyor. About 1700, he
bought property on the southwest corner of the present Tremont and Beacon
Streets, fronting 132 feet on Beacon and 32 on Tremont and containing
a brick house and wooden house. This lot was diagonally opposite King's
Chapel, and is now included in the site of the Tremont Building and therefore
became known as "Melyn's Corner." Jacob died on 11 or 13 December 1706.
His will was dated on 27 September 1706, and was proven on 26 December

being offered for Probate by his widow, Hannah Melyn. It contained specific bequests to his son, Rev. Samuel Melyn and his daughter, Abigail Tilley, wife of William Tilley, Roper Maker, the residue and build of the estate going to his wife Hannah during her life with the reversion divided equally between his son and daughter before mentioned. His wife was name Executrix during her life, and his son and daughter as Executor and Executric respectively after their mother's death. According to the will: [102]

> *I have made my said two children equal in this disposition upon consideration of what I have expended upon my son in the Liberal Education I have given him, over and above what I have since advanced for and bestowed upon him to the value of three hundred pounds and upwards.*

Inventory of this property was made on 25 February 1706 or 1707, by Hannah, showed an estate valued at L 1435 18s 9 d, of which L500 was the value of the real estate. Other interesting items were cash, bills of credit, L654 9s 4d, 76 ounces of plate, L30 8s, Hides, Leather and "35 pair washed leather breeches," L60. He mentioned Dutch and English books and a seal ring. No decipherable impression of the seal has been found. A seal on a letter from Jacob to Jacob Leisler of 11 December 1689 is broken and undecipherable. Therefore, it's unknown if a coat of arms exist. Hannah was buried on 15 November 1717 in Boston.

Generation I

Jacob Melyn and Hannah Hubbard

SUSANNA MELYN, bapt. 3 October 1674, witnesses by Jacob Kip and Susannah Molyn, at the Dutch Church.

JACOB MELYN, bapt. 3 October 1674, witnesses by Jacob Kip and Susannah Molyn, at the Dutch Church.

DANIEL MELYN, bapt. 7 August 1677, witnessed by Isaac Molyn and Hillegond Joris, at the Dutch Church.

REV. SAMUEL MELYN, b. New York about 1675; bapt. 7 August 1677, witnessed by Isaac Molyn and Hillegond Joris, at the Dutch Church; joined in a deed with his parents on 26 May 1697, where he's specifically mentioned as being over 21 years of age; went to Boston with parents in fall of 1684 to be set up as a leather dealer; entered college, placed fifth in class, which he held until after this event that he describes: [103]

. . . Towards the End of our Sophymoreship by my andaciously calling freshmen at the door of the Worthy Mr. brattle in a way of contemept, the Venerable and Reverend President with my Tutor, the well deserving Mr. Leverett saw it convenient to place me the lowest in the class, whereas I was before between Sir Remington and Sir Whitman.

He earned his A.B. degree in 1696. Records show his provisional training was fifth in a class of ten. His formal standing at the end of his freshman year was sixth. The final order at graduation shows him at the foot of a class of nine, one of the original members having been expelled in the meantime. This degradation was a disciplinary measure because Samuel's hazing some freshmen at the end of his sophomore year. An interesting letter from him to the Rev. Cotton Mather, 19 May 1698, where he pleaded to be restored to his former standing before the next catalogue was issued, is among the Massachusetts Archives. His requested was denied. Probably the fact that he had been fined 16s 8d. for the hazing episode (the largest fine imposed in years) and subsequently fined 5s. 3d. and 8s. 6d. for other offenses prevented the granting of his request. Records show that he spent vast sums in commons, frequently more than 4 pounds a quarter. Despite his troubles, he remained at Harvard until October 1696. Two years later he sought to escape the stigma of being entered in the catalogue at the foot of his class. With a letter to Cotton Mather, explaining why he had not returned a borrowed book, he sent: [104]

Now, Sir my humble request is . . . that you would be plead to motion to the Reverend President, that I may be reduced into my former station-Nothing Sir can be more gratefull to my Father and mother, nor any thing more encouraging to me-I am very Sorry (and desire tobe very penitent) that as well as in many other things I have displeased so worthy as Gentleman as the President . . . Had I, Sir! Been placed at first Inferior to the rest, I should have been contented and thought it my place (wherefore Sir I hope you will not conjecture that pride is the Impulsive cause of this my Petition) but it being after such a nature as it was, makes me very desirous of reducement.-Sir all our class that were placed at first beneath me, have voluntarily manifested unto me that they were very willing I should Enjoy my Antient standing.

His request was denied, and at Commencement, 1699, he received his M.A. degree, still at the foot of his class. On this occasion he argued on the negative side of the question: "An Religio vi et Armis sit progaganda?" (Should forcible means be used for the propagation of religion?). He taught school at Hadley, Massachusetts from 1700-1 for which he received 38 l. He was in Elizabeth, New Jersey on 14 December 1702, when he witnessed John Clark's will. He was ordained on 20 May 1704 as the colleague of

John Harriman, pastor of the First Presbyterian Church. [105]

What was spent on the occasion:

per money layd out in sweet spice at N.Y.	3.6
per ¾ bushel of wheat at 4s	3.0
per bushel of barley mault	3.9
per 6 lb of butter	3.0
per 1 qt of rum 15d	1.3
per 3 lb sugr at 6d is	1.6
per pepper 9d is	0.9
per 4 lb cheese	2.0
per qutrs lamb, wt 8 lb ¾ at 4d is	2.11
per 2 qt veal	4.2

Shortly after this, he married, for his old neighbor, Judge Samuel Sewall, who married Samuel's sister, Abigail, recorded in his diary of 23 August 1705 that "Mr. Sam. Melyen and his wife dine with us." As this is the only evidence reference to a wife of Samuel that has been found as Hannah Melyen who died in 1717 was his mother, not his wife (The compiler, through the courtesy of the Massachusetts Historical Society, verified the reference with the original manuscript diary).

Professor Winan's research indicates this will was in Samuel's hands and was proved on 8 June 1705, but he was not one of the provers. It was known that he was in Boston on 23 August 1705 and was quite probably there when the will was proven. He was also a witness to Abraham Hatfield's will at Elizabeth, 8 July 1706.

After Harriman died, Samuel became sole charge of the congregation, but his relations was it were unfortunate. Tradition says that he was suspected of being intemperate, and that soon after he entered the meeting-house one Sunday morning the choir and a tune which he supposed to be intended for his admonition, and that he immediately left the pulpit and with his wife walked out, and never again entered the building.

He preached there until October 1706 and was possibly there as late as January 1708 when he was a delegate to a religious conference at Newark. Later in 1708, the pulpit was reported vacant, but was soon filled by Rev. Jonathan Dickinson, who married about the time to Samuel's cousin, Joanna Melyn. He continued living in Elizabethtown, and served as one of the overseers of the highways. There is a tradition that he was dismissed for some occurrence, possibly intemperance or card playing that cause him to lose the confidence of the congregation. At the Court of Quarter Sessions, held at Elizabeth in November 1710, a complaint was brought against Rev. Samuel and several others, but its nature was never recorded. A true bill was found against him and he was ordered into the custody of the Sheriff until he should give bail. The court session of 21 August 1711 at Newark reported that he had died since the May session

of the Court. His wife must have died before him, for his will mentioned no relatives other than a sister in Boston. To the Jewell family, with whom he seems to have boarded, he left his pewter tumbler and silver spoon, his looking-glass and three "Turkey worked chears," his saddle pillion, books, and bow and arrows.

By deed of 20 April 1704, recorded on 5 June 1705, Samuel purchased from Thomas Sayre and his wife six acres of land adjoining on the north the present Lecture Room of the First Presbyterian Church, on the west side of Broad Street, Elizabeth, and on 7 May 1711, he sold the same property, then described as a "dwelling house, orchard and pasture" to George Jewell. It may be that Samuel remained in this house as a boarder, after its sale to Jewell, who was the Executor, and a beneficiary, of the will of Samuel. This will, of 10 May 1711 and proved 31 July of that year, does not mention any wife or children of the testator. The beneficiaries were his sister Abigail of Boston, several members of the Jewell family, and "Mrs. Anne Gardner," whose relationship (if any) to the testator has not been determined. An interesting side light is the fact that an "Anne Gardner" was one of those indicated with the Rev. in the Court case. The inventory of his estate was taken on 19 July 1711, which was doubtless fairly soon after his death. It mentions among other interesting items a "Library of Books" valued at 85 pounds 1s, also a "great Dutch bible" 2 pounds 10s., and an "English bible, large octavo" 10s.

ABIGAIL MELYN, b. about 1666 as a letter of 23 February 1719/20 from her third husband, Judge Samuel Sewall to Jeremiah Dummer stated that she was then in the 54th year of her age; bapt. 7 August 1677, witnesses by Isaac Molyn and Hillegond Joris at the Dutch Church, same time as her brother, Samuel; undoubtedly went to Boston with her parents and her brother Samuel in fall of 1684; (M1) James Woodmansey 17 May 1686; a Letter of Administration on his estate was issued on Jacob Melyn on 15 March 1693/4 designating him as a shopkeeper; 16 March 1693/4, his widowed submitted an inventory of her late husband's estate showing the value of 19 pounds 5 s. The estate was found to be insolvent and after the usual formalities, the order of distribution was issued on 11 February 1695/6; (M2) William Tilley 27 May 1700, rope maker of Boston; his will mentioned his wife Abigail "*whose father and mother are both dead,*" also his two daughters by a previous marriage, namely Isabella; (M3) Judge Samuel Sewall 29 October 1719, Chief Justice of Massachusetts and too well known due to his famous diary; no children by this marriage; no doubt was the richest man in Province at time of his death; he left no will

and his administrators saw no use in returning an inventory. Amicable partition, no doubt, was sufficient for the heirs. A few days before they were married, they executed an ante nuptial agreement. It provided (in substance) that Samuel settle upon Abigail an annuity of 60 pounds I case she became his widow, and he waived all interest I her real estate except the enjoyment of the rents and use thereof, in return for which Abigail waived her dower rights. A third party to the agreement was Daniel Oliver, who as trustee was to hold Abigail's real estate. This legal device preserved to her, notwithstanding the marriage, separate rights of property, except a life interest in her real estate.

In terms Samuel agreed to forgo any interest that he might have reason of the marriage in her estate other then "*rents, issues and profits of all that her Dwelling house & land thereto belonging with the Out-housing fences members and appurtenances situate in Boston aforesaid near the Church of England, so called, and where of her Hond father Jacob Melyen dyed seized in fee*" which were to go to him during his natural life. The agreement further provided that he (Samuel) would do whatever might be requisite in law to enable her to dispose of her estate in such manner as she might desire, by will or deed. At the end of the agreement a "Memo" was appended to make clear that the income from her real estate as described above was to be paid to Samuel not only after Abigails' death, but also during her lifetime. The whole instrument was executed by Abigail on 27 October 1719 and as signed and acknowledged by her only was recorded on 7 June 1720 a few days after her death, on 26 May 1720. As the other parties to the agreement conveyed no interest in real estate thereby, the duplicate copies presumably executed by them were not recorded.

Abigail died intestate, and the property then passed to her heirs, subject to the life interest of Samuel Sewall. Since she left no surviving children or brothers or sister, the heirs were her first cousins on her father's side, from whom the property came to her. Under the law, as it was at that time, the first cousins were entitled to take to the exclusion of the first cousins one removed; that is, Jacob Melyn's then living nephew and nieces took the exclusion of the children of his deceased nephews and nieces. However, if there were any living at the time of her death, but who later died, their children were entitled to a share in the real estate, by her parents' inheritance; she died on 26 May 1720.

James and Abigail

i. **Elizabeth**, bapt. 10 April 1687; d. young.
ii. **JACOB**, b. 1 March 1694; d. aged 10 years.

Isaac Melyn (II)

Isaack Melyn II, the youngest child of the Melyn immigrants, was born and baptized on 22 July 1646 in the Dutch Reformed Church of New Amsterdam as "Isaac Molyn" which was witnessed by Hendrick Coop and Lijntje Jochems. He was injured in the Indian Massacre in 1655.

New York

Isaack grew up and became a long resident of New York. He was sentenced to a 5 pound fine and imprisoned until a 20-pound bond was paid (by his brother, Jacob, on 26 December) for "inveiglement" (seduction) of John Davenport's servant girl, Hester Clark. Just south of the houses, owned by Jacob when their mother passed, along Broad Street, was a small space of ground that once belonged to the Melyn's and became available for building when the Heere Graft was opened and regulated about 1657. A cottage was built here and this is where Isaac lived.

New Haven, Connecticut

In several pages of handwritten material of 1 December 1663, relate what must have been one of the sensational Blue Law cases that straitlaced this New England town. Hest Clark was the orphan daughter of John Clark and her legal guardian was Nicholas Elsie. At the time of this incident, Hester was maid servant in the family of the Reverend John Davenport, a founder of New Haven, and one of the "seven pillars" of New Haven's civil government. Isaac, then between 17 and 18 years of age, was charged with inveigling Hester Clark's affections; with having carried her forth in the night double on a horse (having a bottle of strong liquor with him) after the Davenport family was in bed; with having (at her invitation) spent three hours in her bedchamber;

165

and with having a "diabolical art to draw mayde's affections." Through the investigation, a number of other young men and women were more or less involved in the escapade, which apparently was thoroughly enjoyed by all the participants. The court fined Isaac 5 pounds, and ordered to be imprisoned until security was given for his good behavior in a bond of 20 pounds. This was done on 26 December 1663, which was guaranteed by Samuel van Godenhuysem. Hester Clark was fined 3 pounds, "and was seriously warned to take heed she be not taken in any sinful ways again."

New York

After the breaking up of the Melyn home in New Haven, he returned to New York and in 1671, formed a partnership with Captain Thomas Delavall. New York was in English possession and Isaac was granted letters of denization "anew" to be "a Free Denizen of this Place & Province" on 13 January 1671/2. Here Isaac was recorded as being a Commander and part owner of the ship Expectatie. [106]

16 September 1671

Edward Randall, Plt, v/s isacq Melyn, Deft. The Plt. Declared that this Deft became indebted unto the Plt. By his bill, in the sume of L 14: 00: 6. Sterling to bee paid in New Yorke provisions, and delivered in Barbados fraigt ffree, and more for wages of this Plt. Servant the sume of L 12: 13: 4: for which said debts the Plt. Craves Judgement against the def. With Cost of Suit. The def. Owes the debt of L 14: 00: 06. But sayeth hee Left in the Plt. Handes 80 deal boards and 13 Sparres for to dispose of for the defts account at Barbados. Uppon hearing of ye debates of bothe parties; ye Court ordered the deft. To give to the plt. Security ffor the payment of the sd. Debt of L 14: 0: 6. At Barbadoes; provided the Plt. Likewise gives in Security for to bee Accomptable to ye. Deft for the sale of the deal boards and spares; abd about the wages of the plts Servant, the Court thought fitt to Referre the Same unto the determination of Mr. Jacocb Kip & Mr. Thomas Williams this afternoone.

On 24 October 1671, a number of men "being in much liquor" went on board this vessel while it was at anchor in the harbor, and attempted to seize it, alleging that it was "a Dutch bottom" whereupon the Executive Council ordered an investigation, as a result of which it was adjudged to be a "free vessel" and Governor Lovelace allowed it to clear, a pass being granted to sail to Nevis in the West Indies. [107-109]

9 November 1671

Att a Speciall Court of Mayor & Alderm. Held at New Yorke the 9th Day of November, 1671 ... Mr. Isaack Melyn ... appeared as a juror.

24 July 1672

James Sparr beeeing examined in Court about the Oproar Committed by him & companie, answered what he hath done he did it only by Misinformation of the Mate of Isaacq Malyns Shipp, who had advised him that it was a dutch bottom; but humbly Craves pardon for what he did. Humphrey Davenpoort being Likewise Examined saith that he was verry much in drinckc and doth not remember how he came on board; Neither Knew of No harme. Henry Randel being Examined what he had to do on board in Seizing the Ship of Isaacq Melyn & Landing of the Gunns. And answered that he only followed the order of his Commander, James Spragg. The Court ordered that the s (d) James Spragg, Humphrey davenport & jenry Randel should be released of their only giving in sedurity for their appearance at the Court of Oyer & Terminer to be held on Thursday next.

To the Magistrates & Officers at New haerlem.
New Yorke Septembr 17th 1672.

Uppon Hearing off the difference betweene Mr. Isacq Melyn and his mate henry Ridger The Worp. Mayer did ffind and Order that the s (d) Mr. Melyn shall pay unto his dais mate wages at the Rate of three pound per month until the first day of September the s (d) Melyn making appeare by his booke hee entered him soo; or otherwise to pay three pound & ten Shilling per Month deducting for the Indigo three Shillings pr lb. & for ye. Coate fourthy five gilders: But Concerning ye s(d). Rodgers pretence of seven day days which Capt. Wever & five Shillings about Klearing of ye ship at Neevis is not allouwed of.

2 November 1672:

The Expectatie started for Barbadoes, but on the second day out was forced to turn back because it was leaking, and there was a possibility that the cargo would be damaged. Isaac petitioned the Executive Council on the 19th, and the Council appointed four men (one being Jacob Leisler) to compose the difference between the freighters and the Command if possible. Three days later, since the matter couldn't be disposed of, Isaac was authorized to unload the vessel, and arbitrators were selected by both sides to determine the extent of the damages.

5 September 1673:

In the case in question between Jan Romyn and Sander Leendersen, pltfs, v/s Isaack melyn, deft., the W. Court selected and appointed as arbitrators Sieur Jacob Lyslaer, Dirck van Cleef and Thomas Williams, who are requested to hear the differences between parties and if possible to reconcile them; otherwise to report to the Court.

The Schout, Burgomasters and Schepens further resolved and concluded that the tapsters outside of this place be allowed to lay in a barrel of strong beer at Burgher excise at harvest or the Merry Making and at burials both within and without this City according as that Schouot Burgomasters and Schepens shall order on similar occasions.

Item, all officers belonging to the Fort William Hendrick must pay the full excise as well as the tapsters themselves, if they lay I and consume any wines or beer in tapsters house.

Item, the payment of the excise shall be collected and pad forthwith if possible; otherwise within the time of fourteen days.

On 11 September 1673, New York being then in possession of the Dutch, the Council of War resolved that the late English governor Lovelace must depart forthwith for New England, or for Holland, in the *Expectatie*, then about to sail. Lovelace, however, asked that he might be allowed to go to Holland "in Commander Benckes' ship" and his request was granted. The *Expectatie* on its outbound voyage, lost its mast and sails in a heavy storm off Nantucket, and was seized as a prize by Captain Thomas Dudson (or Dodson), and taken to Boston. The first of a long series of lawsuits was soon begun, and the case continued in litigation for a long time. Boston and Plymouth colonies each claimed jurisdiction over the case, and on 29 September 1674 Charles the Second ordered the authorities at Boston to send the vessel to England for adjudication of the case. This was apparently not done, and the final outcome of the suit is not known. Several secondary suits were started, and the matter of the *Expectatie* became a somewhat celebrated case of maritime law.

New York

Isaac returned to New York during the final hearings of his case, on 8 May 1674. The news of the Treat of Westminster was then known in New England, but had not been made public in New York, although rumors of it had reached the authorities there. Isaac told some Dutchmen who had come to his house of the promised surrender. This news spread quickly in New York and there was an open rebellion against Governor Colve for the apparent concealment of the real facts. And so on 12 May 1674, Isaac was sentenced "to come personally every day, when the Burger companies are employed at the City fortifications, and work with them until said fortifications be completed." [110-111]

11 September 1674 (1673), a Court of Schout, Burgomasters and Schepens holden in the City Hall of the City N: Orange:

Jan Romyn, pltf. v/s Isaack Melyn, deft. Pltf. Demanding from deft. A barrel of floour and three bushels of peas, offers to confirm the same on oath. Deft. Says, he knows nothing about it and offers in like manner to confirm his assertion on oath. Burgomasters and Schepens asked both parties, if they will submit the case in question to the Court as arbitrators? Both answer, Yes. Whereupon the W. Burgomasters and Schepens as arbitrators adjudged, that the deft. Shall pay the pltf. 24 shillings and 9 (d) old English money or the value thereof payment in provisions at four for one.

James Mattheus, ltlf. v/s Isack Melyn, deft. Pltf. Claims, that there is due him by a/c the sum of fl. 1210. 3. And requests, that the deft. Be ordered to pay him before he leaves here. Deft. says that the pltf. May swear to his ac as far as concerns his particulars a/c/ and is then willing to pay, but he refuses to pay, what the seamen have disbursed. Order, that the private a/c be paid, and further at the reques of parties, the Court have as arbitrators regarding the debt of the sailors, resolved that the deft. shall

pay the pltf. Instead of fl. 594. 10. In question, the sum of f. 325 only.
Against this the deft. brings in that he has paid a/c the sum of fl. 1092,
which the pltf. Admits; so that the deft. remains indebted to the pltf. By
balance the sum of fl. 443. 3., which he, the deft., shall pay to the pltf.
Before his departure or otherwise give satisfactory security.

He was still a prisoner on 27 September 1674 when he addressed a long petition to Governor Colve praying to be released (date unknown). Since Colve officially surrendered New York to the English on 10 November, he could have been release soon after. In September 1678, Isaac was accused of breaking into the house of Henry Newton (City Marshal) and knocked him down, striking him to the ground with his first on 24 August.

He had sold the ship, *Expectatie*, in 1722, by Joanna, Jonathan Dickson's wife, of Elizabethtown, who was the only surviving child of Isaac, to Willaim Verplanck, a New York merchant. He (M1) Dorothea Samson before 1679. On 6 July 1680, Jacob France bought suit against Jacob claiming that his wife had nursed Isaac Melyn's child for one and quarter years and declared for L18 10s "at the rate of 600 guilders per anno, one half to be paid in money and one half in Long Island wheat." The case was withdrawn. The mother, Dorothea, may have died at childbirth as Isaac remarried on 5 October 1679 to Temperance Loveridge.

On 21 September 1680, Isaac was granted a liquor license where he was an inn holder. On occasion, he would bring his vessel from New York to the harbor that his sister, Cornelia, lived. One of his receipts for freight for the return voyage is still extant., "one board the barke, 25 May, 1680 and he took with him "tobacco pips," from the fields of Easthampton, linen and woolen from its domestic manufactures, whalebone and oil from the fisheries, and the unsold remainder apparently of a mercantile shipment, from William Darvall, "Sarge and Cersey", and gunpowder. On 6 September 1681, he brought suit against "Abraham Corbett and others, Farmers and Excise" claiming that they had entered his house and cellar and abused his wife. One witness said he saw a man take Mrs. Melyn by the arm. The Court found for Isaac.

The Farmers of the Excise filed for a counterclaim against Isaac about April 1682, but the result is not known. The Isaac went into an agreement with a Grederick Phillipse on 4 December 1682 about a voyage to be made to a Spanish wreck on the Bahama Islands. On 4 September 1683, William Robinson filled a complaint of assault and batter against Isaac and witnesses were produced to show Isaac had broken his leg.

Isaack's last years were spent in Elizabeth City County, Virginia, not far from the present city of Hampton. The exact year is not known but sometime between 1684 and 1688, a certificate for 500 acres of land was issued to William Earle, for the importation into the colony of fire persons, one of whom was Isaack. They show that Isaack, his negro woman Tema or Tena, and three workmen, with their freight, were brought from New England to Virginia, where Melyn erected a saw mill and a grist mill on the head of the Back River, a little north and west of Hampton. The money for the transportation of the party and their belongings was advanced by Bertram Servant, who is mentioned in Bruce's *Social Life of Virginia* as "a wealthy planter of French origin." On 16 June 1688, Isaac entered into an agreement with Bertram Servant under the terms of which Servant was authorized to take over the saw and grist mills and to manage them at his discretion so that he might obtain reimbursement for the money which Isaac owned him for the transportation and also for money owned for provisions and for material for the work of the mills. Servant was also to have fourteen per cent of the earnings of the mills. The matter was brought into Court on 18 November 1689 by Servant because of the failure of Melyn to comply with the terms of the agreement. Servant had claimed that there was due him 29 pounds 6s. 6d. on account of his disbursements and "5496 foot of several sorts of plank," 4 bushels of wheat and 31 bushels, 3 pecks of Indian Corn, being fourteen per cent of the output of the mills. Judgment was rendered against Melyn, which not being paid, his estate was ordered seized on 18 December 1689, and the execution of the order was reported to the Court on the following day.

The Elizabeth City County Records has a reference of no date to the granting of a certificate to Isaack for the land. Presumably it was upon this land tract that he erected the saw and grist mills. The compiler fond on a loose sheet of paper stuck between the leaves of a record book a deposition by Thomas Walterson, a former employee of Isaac, which goes at great length into the technique of operating a grist mill, and relates how Melyn would only allow coarse meal to be ground, but that he [Walterson] would privately set the mill so that it would grind fine meal. On such occasions if Melyn came into the mill, "he would sweare curse and imidiately alter the mill." Walterson also stated that Melyn had pulled down the first mill which he had erected and replaced it with an inferior one.

On 27 January 1692/3, Isaack was a defendant when Captain Anthony Armistead brought charges against him for trespass. It would seem that Armistead owned land adjacent to that on Melyn's mill land, and that Melyn had extended his operations onto Armistead's land. Melyn claimed that the work was done on his own land, so a jury was empanelled and a survey ordered to settle the suit, on 8 May 1683, and the decision being that the land belonged to Armistead. Melyn filed an appeal but it was never decided because Isaack died on 18 May 1693. The estate inventory was taken on the 19ᵗʰ, which mentioned 1 old sea compass, 1 quadrant and veynes, 1 large "Byble," 3 Dutch books, 2 old periwigs and 1 broad cloth lined coat. As the inventory lists only one bedstead, with the corresponding amount of bedding, it would seem that there were few, if any, members of his family with him at the time of his death.

An interesting side light is the petition of Benjamin Dodd, "late servant unto Mr. Isaac Melyen, deceased, having duly served his tie according to indenture' that he be given the customary grant of clothing, which petition was allowed and Pascho Curle was ordered to give him "a new Carsey Coat and breeches and a Capp, 2 shirts of blew linen, and one pair of new shoes and stocking," the cost of these to be charged to the estate.

It was mentioned that Isaac Melyn received a grant of land bringing eighteen persons into the Colony of Virginia. Of these persons, who are named, some can be identified as workmen of servants. The members of the Melyn family are named in the following order: Isaac, Ryderus, Temperance (who may have been Isaac Melyn's wife or a daughter), Johannah, Isaac, Junior and Robert. All of these can be placed except for Robert. The fact that he is mentioned last would seem to indicate either that he was the youngest child or that he was a more distant relative. There is a reference in the Calendar of State papers of 26 November 1684, to a quarrel which occurred on 31 October on the ketch Quaker, at that time in Chesapeake Bay, to which quarrel one "Robert Moline" was a witness. Isaac could not have had a son who was old enough to testify in 1684, so if this Robert was related to Isaac, t must have been in a collateral line. Except that both persons were named Robert, and that the incident occurred in the general neighborhood where Isaac *may* have been at the time, there is nothing to indicate that the separate references are to the same person, Isaac died in Virginia in 1693 where on 7 July, his son Riderus receives his Uncle Jacob Melyn, of Boston, as guardian.

Isaac and Dorothea		iii.	Temperance
		iv.	Joanna
i.	Riderus	v.	Isaack
ii.	Dorothea	vi.	Robert

Isaac and Temperance

GENERATION I

Isaac Melyn and Dorothea Samson

RIDERUS MELYN, b. before July 1679, since he must have been at least 14 years old to be allowed to choose his own guardian since "Riderus Melyen, son of Isaac Melyen, late of Virginia Planter, dec'd, being a minor" did on 27 July 1693 where he appeared before the Judge of Probate in Boston and made choice of his "well respected Uncle, Jacob Melyen, of Boston in the County of Suffolk in New England, Leather Seller" to be his guardian and on 19 March 1693/4 in the Court at Elizabeth City County, Virginia. Pascho Curle was made administrator of Isaac's estate "in behalfe of Ryderus Melyen, son and heir of Isaac Melyen, dec'd." On 19 October 1696, Curle, who had been summoned (by order of Court held 18 May 1696) to render an account of the estate of profits of the mill, answered that he "ought not to render account to this Court for that he hath a Power of Attorney from the Orphan's guardian, and will produce the same at the next Court." Records show that this was not done and though there are many references to this case, it was still pending at the end of 1699, when the record closes. He died before 13 June 1722, his half sister, Joanna Dickinson described herself in a deed as "the only surviving child of Isaac Melyen, late of the Citty of New York, mariner, deceased."

DOROTHEA MELYN, bapt. 12 April 1679 in Dutch Church with witnesses Jacob Molyn and Hendrickje ver Planken.

Isaac Melyn and Temperance Loveridge

TEMPERANCE MELYN, mentioned in a land grant to Isaac Melyn.

JOANNA MELYN, b. 1682; bapt. as "Jannetie" in the New York Dutch Church on 24 May 1682 with witnesses Jacob Molyn and Geertruyd Schuyler; m. Rev. Jonathan Dickinson, Yale graduate 1706; 29 September 1709, ordained a pastor of Presbyterian Church, succeeding Rev. Samuel Melyn; first president of College of New Jersey, later becoming Princeton University, a hall erected there in 1870 to commemorate his name; d. 20 April 1745 and therefore, the last survivor of descendant of Cornelius Melyn; he d. 7 October 1747 and buried Presbyterian Church Yard, Elizabeth, New Jersey; his will of 16 September 1747 and proved on 13 October which mentioned his wife and children except his son Melyen and daughter, Joanna.

    i.   Melyen
   ii.   Abigail
  iii.   Jonathan
  iv.   Temperance
   v.   Joanna
  vi.   Elizabeth
 vii.   Mary
viii.   Martha

ISAAC MELYN, bapt. 30 May 1684 Dutch Church with Isaac van Vleck and Geesje Barents as witnesses.

ROBERT MELYN, mentioned in a land grant to Isaac Melyn.

GENERATION II

Jonathan Dickinson and
Joanna Melyn

MELYEN DICKINSON b. 7 December 1709; d. 6 January 1710.

ABIGAIL DICKINSON, b. 16 June 1711; m. Jonathan Sergeant 1745, merchant, surveyor, Treasurer of College of New Jersey, his house here was on site of the present Nassau Club; their great-grandson, Jonathan, submitted Melyn manuscripts to NY Historical Society.

    i.   Jonathan

JONATHAN DICKINSON, b. 19 September 1713 Hatfield, Massachusetts; m. Joanna Melyn; 1731 Yale Graduate; mentioned in Yale Catalogue in 1763 as "dead".

TEMPERANCE DICKINSON, b. 11 May 1715; m. John Odell.

    i.   Jonathan

JOANNA DICKINSON, b. 27 February 1717; d. 9 May 1732; buried Elizabeth, New Jersey, "Mrs." on stone.

ELIZABETH DICKINSON, b. 3 March 1721 Hartford, Connecticut; m. Jonathan Ross Miller; d. 29 November 1788.

    i.   Abigail
    ii. Capt. Melyn
    iii. Sarah
    iv. Sarah
    v. Moses
    vi. Jonathan
    vii. Elizabeth

MARY DICKINSON, b. 15 October 1722; (M1) John Cooper; (M2) Plum of Neward, New Jersey; d. 1763-4.

MARTHA DICKINSON, b. 18 May 1725; m. Rev. Caleb Smith 7 September 1748; d. 20 August 1757; Rev. was first tutor in College of New Jersey, class of 1743, Trustee 1750 and pro tem President.

    i.   Anna
    ii. Elizabeth
    iii. Jane

GENERATION III

*Jonathan Sergeant and
Abigail Dickinson*

(HON.) JONATHAN SERGEANT, b. 1746 Neward, New Jersey; (M1) Margaret Spencer 14 March 1775; (M2) Elizabeth Rittenhouse 20 December 1788; B. S., College of New Jersey, 1762; B. S., College of Philadelphia (now University of Pennsylvania), 1763; d. 8 October 1793 Philadelphia of yellow fever; buried Laurel Hill Cemetery, Philadelphia.

Jonathan and Margaret

i.   William
ii.   Sarah
iii.   John
iv.   Thomas
v.   Elihu Spencer
vi.   ?
vii.   ?
viii. ?

Jonathan and Elizabeth

ix.   Esther
x.   David
xi.   Frances

*John Odell and
Temperance Dickinson*

JONATHAN ODELL, b. 25 September 1737 Newark, New Jersey; clergyman; College of New Jersey, 1754, studied medicine and served as surgeon in British army; resigned and went to England, ordained deacon 21 December 1766, in Chapel Royal of St. James Palace; 1767, advanced to Priest's orders; returned to states 1767, became rector of St. Ann's (now St. Mary's) Church in Burlington, New Jersey during Revolution; d. 25 November 1818 Fredericton, New Brunswick.

i.   William Franklin

*Jonathan Miller and
Elizabeth Dickinson*

ABIGAIL MILLER, m. Daniel Baker 30 September 1756 New Jersey.

i.   Elizabeth
ii.   Melyn
iii.   Phoebe
iv.   Abigail
v.   Daniel
vi.   Joanna
vii.   Jonathan
viii. Miller
ix.   Peter

CAPTAIN MELYN MILLER

SARAH MILLER

SARAH MILLER

MOSES MILLER

JONATHAN MILLER

ELIZABETH MILLER

Caleb Smith and Martha Dickinson

ANNA SMITH, b. 27 June 1749;
m. George Green 4 May 1769; d.
1789.

i.   Caleb
ii. Charles
iii. James
iv. Richard Montgomery
v.   Anna

ELIZABETH SMITH, b. 27 November
1752

JANE SMITH, b. 28 September 1755.

GENERATION IV

*Jonathan Sergeant and
Margaret Spencer*

WILLLIAM SERGEANT, b. 1 January 1776; m. Elizabeth Morgan; 1792, University of Pennsylvania; attorney; d. 7 March 1807.

SARAH SERGEANT, m. Samuel Miller.

HON. JOHN SERGEANT, b. 5 December 1779 Philadelphia, Pennsylvania; bapt. 23 January 1780 First Presbyterian Church; m. Margaret Watmough; US Congress; d. 25 November 1852 Philadelphia; buried Laurel Hill Cemetery, Philadelphia; she d. 4 April 1869 and buried with him.

    i.   John
    ii.   Margaretta
    iii. Anna
    iv. Sarah
    v.   Spencer M.D.
    vi. Ellen
    vii. Maria
    viii. John
    ix. Katherine
    x.   William

THOMAS SERGEANT, b. 1782; d. 1860.

ELIHU SPENCER SERGEANT, b. 1787; attorney.

*Jonathan Sergeant and
Elizabeth Rittenhouse*

ESTHER SERGEANT, b. 1789; m. Dr. W.P.C. Barton; d. 1870.

DAVID SERGEANT, b. 1791; d. 1872.

FRANCES SERGEANT, b. 1793; m. John C. Lowber; d. 1847.

William Odell

WILLIAM FRANKLIN ODELL, b. 19 October 1774 Burlington, New Jersey; succeeded his father as provincial secretary of New Brunswick in 1812; hired by British commissioners in 1817-8 to survey and locate boundaries between New Brunswick and states under treat of Gent; d. 25 December 1844 Frederickton, New Brunswick.

    i.   William Hunter

Daniel Baker and Abigail Miller

ELIZABETH BAKER, b. 17 December 1757 Elizabeth, New Jersey; d. 6 December 1814 Elizabeth, New Jersey; buried Connecticut Farms Churchyard, Section II, Row L, Union, New Jersey.

MELYN BAKER, b. 10 January 1760 Elizabeth, New Jersey; m. Prudence Whitehead 19 February 1786 New

Jersey; d. 20 January 1826 Mad River, Clark County, Ohio; buried Enon Cemetery, Enon, Ohio.

    i.   Elizabeth
    ii.   Elias
    iii.   Daniel
    iv.   Melyn D.
    v.   Ezra Dickenson
    vi.   Phoebe B.

PHOEBE BAKER, b. 31 December 1761; m. Moses Miller 3 December 1780; d. 4 November 1813.

ABIGAIL BAKER, b. February 1764 Elizabeth, New Jersey.

DANIEL BAKER, b. 23 February 1766 Elizabeth, New Jersey; m. Rebecca Headley; d. 26 August 1828 Union, New Jersey; both buried Connecticut Farms Churchyard, New Jersey.

    i.   Phebe
    ii.   Elizabeth
    iii.   Daniel
    iv.   Maria
    v.   Oliver

JOANNA BAKER, b. 21 August 1768 Elizabeth, New Jersey; d. September 1783.

JONATHAN BAKER, b. 23 October 1770 Elizabeth, New Jersey; m. Sarah Mulford; d. 18 March 1841 Clark County, Ohio.

    i.   Moses M.

MILLER BAKER, b. 25 March 1773 Elizabeth, New Jersey; m. Sarah Winans; d. 10 May 1810; buried Connecticut Farms Churchyard, Section II, Row L, New Jersey.

PETER BAKER, b. 25 March 1783 Elizabeth, New Jersey; m. Mary Rosanna Ortman; d. 1848.

George Green and Anna Smith

CALEB GREEN, b. 2 July 1770; m. Elizabeth Van Cleve; d. 1850.

    i.   Caleb
    ii.   Charles Dickinson
    iii.   James H.
    iv.   Richard Montgomery
    v.   Matilda

CHARLES GREEN, b. 28 November 1771; class of 1787; d. 1857.

JAMES H. GREEN, b. January 1774; d. 1801.

RICHARD MONTGOMERY GREEN, b. 6 November 1775; Class of 1794; m. Mary Henderson; d. 1853.

    i.   Matilda

ANNA GREEN, m. M. Benjamin Van Cleve 20 September 1786.

    i.   George

GENERATION V

John Sergeant and Margaret Watmoug

John Sergeant, b. 1822; d. 23 July 1856.

Margaretta Sergeant, b. 26 June 1814; m. Gen. George Gordon Meade 31 December 1840 St. Peter's Church, Pennsylvania; he was a Major General in Army as commander at Battle of Gettysburg; d. 7 January 1886.

Anna Sergeant, b. 10 June 1815; m. Benjamin Gerhard; d. 21 June 1873.

Sarah Sergeant, b. 24 September 1817; m. Henry Alexander Wise November 1840 Philadelphia; d. 14 October 1850 Accomack Co, Virginia.

Spencer Sergeant, M.D., b. 1827; d. 24 June 1851.

Ellen Sergeant, b. 1831; d. 19 April 1902; single.

Maria Sergeant, b. 17 January 1820; m. Harrison Smith 29 June 1854; d. 25 May 1908.

John Sergeant, b. 1821; d. 1822.

Katherine Sergeant, b. 1825; m. Henry A. Cram; d. 1909.

    i.   John
    ii. Harry

William Sergeant, b. 29 August 1829; m. Eliza Lawrence Espy; d. 11 April 1865.

William Odell

William Hunter Odell, b. 26 November 1811 New Brunswick; 1832 King's College, Fredericton; admitted into bar in 1838, appointed clerk of supreme court, New Brunswick, which he resigned in the same year of being appointed deputy provincial secretary registrar and clerk of executive council; judge of court of common pleas in 1847; member of legislative council of New Brunswick by royal warrant in 1850 where he sat till the union; member of the executive council of New Brunswick and postmaster-general from 1865-6; May 1867, called to Dominion senate by royal proclamation.

Melyn Baker and Prudence Whitehead

Elizabeth Baker, b. 2 January 1787; m. John Layton 1805 Clark Co., Ohio; 20 November 1864 Ohio.

ELIAS BAKER, b. 20 December 1788; d. 10 February 1848.

DANIEL BAKER.

MELYN D. BAKER, b. 18 May 1793 Hamilton Co., Ohio; (M1) Margaret McClure 5 September 1822 Clark Co., Ohio; (M2) Mary Layton; d. 4 January 1844.

Melyn and Margaret

 i. Lucinda

Melyn and Mary

 ii. Melyn
 iii. (female)
 iv. Joseph
 v. Elias

EZRA DICKENSON BAKER, b. 1 September 1796 Hamilton Co., Ohio; m. Ann Morgan 27 August 1825 Clark Co., Ohio; d. 11 May 1882.

 i. Alonza

PHOEBE B. BAKER, b. 14 June 1807; m. William Collom 12 October 1828 Clark Co., Ohio; d. 23 September 1885.

Daniel Baker and Rebecca Headley

PHEBE BAKER, b. 31 December 1761 Elizabeth, New Jersey; m.

Moses Miller 3 December 1780; d. 4 November 1813.

 i. Melyn
 ii. Dayton

ELIZABETH BAKER, b. 1796 New Jersey

DANIEL BAKER, b. 5 March 1791 Hamilton Co., Ohio; m. Nancy (Agnes) Snodgrass 17 March 1817 Clark Co., Ohio; d. 21 May 1868 Clark Co., Ohio.

 i. Elizabeth
 ii. Asa D.
 iii. Samuel
 iv. Agnes
 v. Daniel

MARIA BAKER, b. 1802 New Jersey

OLIVER BAKER, b. 1814 New Jersey; m. Margaret Foster Campbell 1 January 1855 New Jersey; d. 22 October 1858 New Jersey.

Jonathan Baker and Sarah Mulford

MOSES M. BAKER, b. 8 August 1909 Clark Co., Ohio; m. Mary about 1834 Clark Co., Ohio; d. 14 August 1881 Clark Co., Ohio.

 i. Robert D.
 ii. Sarah M.
 iii. Miriam

    iv.   Jasper N.
    v.   Jonathan

George Green and Anna Smith

CALEB GREEN SR., b. 1770; m. Elizabeth Van Cleve; d. 1850.

    i.   George
    ii.   John
    iii.   Henry
    iv.   Caleb Jr.

CHARLES DICKINSON GREEN, b. 1771; class of 1787.

JAMES H. GREEN, b. 1774; d. 1801.

RICHARD MONTGOMERY GREEN, b. 1775; class of 1794; m. Mary Henderson; d. 1853.

MATILDA GREEN, b. 1818; m. Samuel McClintock Hamill; d. 1903.

Footnotes

1   Paul Gibson Burton, "The Antwerp Ancestry of Cornelis Melyn," *New York Genealogical and Biographical Record*, Vol. 67 (1936) 252-3.

2   Dr. Jan Kupp and Dr. Simon Hart, *The Early Cornelis Melyn and the Illegal Fur Trade*. 8, 15.

3   Ibid, 15.

4   "Lord and Manors of NY." *The New York Genealogical & Biographical Record* (New York: 1908).

5   *Melyn Papers, 1640-1699* (The Cornell University Library Digital Collection, 1993) 98-99.

6   Ibid, 97-8.

7   "Adriaen Pieterszen Van Alcmaer," *The New York Genealogical and Biographical Record*, Vol 7 (New York: 1876) 117-8.

8   *Melyn Papers, 1640-1699* (The Cornell University Library Digital Collections, 1993) 101-102.

9   Diana Gale Matthiesen, "Deed for Staten Island, 1640 [Cornelis Melyn]," *The Melyn Papers, 1640-1699* (New York: New York Historical Society, 1914) 100-1.

10 Paul Gibson Burton, "Cornelis Melyn, Patroon of Staten Island and Some of His Descendants," *The New York Genealogical & Biographical Record*, Vol. 68. (New York: 1937) 6.

11 Ibid 6

12 Frank Baker, *Baker Ancestry: The Ancestry of Samuel Baker, of Pleasant Valley, Steuben County, New York, with Some of His Descendants* (Chicago: self-published, 1914) 28.

13 Ibid 28.

14 John Fiske, *The Dutch and Quaker Colonies in America* (Boston and New York: Houghton Mifflin: 1902) 223-4.

15 Ibid, 224.

16   Ibid, 224-5.

17   J. H. Inns, *New Amsterdam and Its People* (New York: Charles Scribner's Sons: 1902) 105.

18   Ibid, 106.

19   Ibid, 107.

20   Betty Burt, *The Life and Times of Cornelis Melyn 1600-1674 Patroon of Staten Island New Netherland* (self published).

21   Russell Shorto, *The Island at the Center of the World* (New York: Vintage Books, April 2005) 177.

22   Henry G. Bayer, *The Belgiums: First Settlers in New York and in the Middle States* (Heritage Books, Inc.: 1987) 341.

23   Russell Shorto. *The Island at the Center of the World* (New York: Vintage Books, April 2005) 178.

24   *Broad Advice To The United Netherland Provinces . . . Made and Arranged, From Divers True and Trusty Memoirs, New-York Historical Society* (The Cornell University Library Digital Collections, 1993) NOTE.

25   Ibid, 267-8.

26   Ibid, 268.

27   Ibid, 268-9.

28   Diana Gale Matthiesen, *http://dgmweb.net/genealogy/45/Melyn/Melyn Home. htm.*

29   J. H. Inns, *New Amsterdam and Its People* (New York: Charles Scribner's Sons: 1902) 114.

30   *Melyn Papers, 1640-1699* (The Cornell University Library Digital Collection, 1993) 102-5.

31   Ibid, 105-6

32   Diana Gale Matthiesen, "Agreement between Cornelis Melyn and Lord Nederhorst," *The Melyn Papers, 1640-1699* (New York: New York Historical Society, 1914) 98-99.

33   *Broad Advice To The United Netherland Provinces . . . Made and Arranged, From Divers True and Trusty Memoirs, New-York Historical Society* (The Cornell University Library Digital Collections, 1993) 270.

34   Russell Shorto. *The Island at the Center of the World* (New York: Vintage Books, April 2005) 197.

35   Ibid, 199.

36   Ibid, 200.

37   Ibid, 200.

38   Ibid, 201.

39   Ibid, 202.

40 *Broad Advice to the United Netherland Provinces . . . Made and Arranged, From Divers True and Trusty Memoirs, New-York Historical Society* (The Cornell University Library Digital Collections, 1993) 270-271.

41 Russell Shorto. *The Island at the Center of the World* (New York: Vintage Books, April 2005) 202.

42 Ibid, 202.

43 Ibid, 203.

44 Diana Gale Matthiesen, *http://dgmweb.net/genealogy/45/Melyn/Bios/ Jochem KuyterCornelis Melynin-NN.htm*

45 Henry G. Steinmeyer, *Staten Island 1524-1898* (New York: The Staten Island Historical Society, 1950) 9.

46 *Broad Advice to the United Netherland Provinces . . . Made and Arranged, From Divers True and Trusty Memoirs, New-York Historical Society* (The Cornell University Library Digital Collections, 1993) 273.

47 Frank Baker, *Baker Ancestry: The Ancestry of Samuel Baker, of Pleasant Valley, Steuben County, New York, with Some of His Descendants* (Chicago: self-published, 1914) 32.

48 Diana Gale Matthiesen, "The Cuyter-Melyn Mandamus of 28 Apr 1648," *The Melyn Papers, 1640-1699* (New York: New York Historical Society, 1914) 102-6.

49 Frank Baker, *Baker Ancestry: The Ancestry of Samuel Baker, of Pleasant Valley, Steuben County, New York, with Some of His Descendants* (Chicago: self-published, 1914) 32.

50 J. H. Inns, *New Amsterdam and Its People* (New York: Charles Scribner's Sons, 1902) 116-7.

51 "Cornelis Melyn, Patroon of Staten Island and Some of His Descendants," *New York Genealogical & Biographical Record*, Vol. 68 (New York: 1937) 9.

52 Frank Baker, *Baker Ancestry: The Ancestry of Samuel Baker, of Pleasant Valley, Steuben County, New York, with Some of His Descendants* (Chicago: self-published, 1914) 33-34.

53 Ibid, 35-36.

54 Berthold Ferrow, *Records of New Amsterdam 1653-74*, (Baltimore: Gen. Pub. Co., 1976) 185-6.

55 Ibid, 256.

56 Ibid, 297.

57 Ibid, 315.

58 Ibid, 318.

59 Ibid, 322.

60 Ibid, 323-4.

61   Ibid, 327.

62   Ibid, 330.

63   Ibid, 410.

64   *Melyn Papers, 1640-1699* (The Cornell University Library Digital Collection, 1993) 108-9

65   Berthold Ferrow, *Records of New Amsterdam 1653-74* (Baltimore: Gen. Pub. Co., 1976) 416.

66   Diana Gale Matthiesen, "Power of Attorney by Janneken Melyen, 6 Apr 1656," *The Melyn Papers, 1640-1699* (New York: New York Historical Society, 1914) 108.

67   Berthold Ferrow, *Records of New Amsterdam 1653-74* (Baltimore: Gen. Pub. Co., 1976) 185-6.

68   Ibid, 10.

69   Ibid, 11.

70   Ibid, 48-9.

71   Ibid, 89.

72   "Cornelis Melyn, Patroon of Staten Island and Some of His Descendants," *New York Genealogical & Biographical Record*, Vol. 68 (New York: 1937) 11.

73   Berthold Ferrow, *Records of New Amsterdam 1653-74* (Baltimore: Gen. Pub. Co., 1976) 203.

74   *Melyn Papers, 1640-1699. Cornelis Melyn.* (The Cornell University Library Digital Collection, 1993) 123.

75   Paul Gibson Burton, "Cornelis Melyn, Patroon of Staten Island and Some of His Descendants," *The New York Genealogical & Biographical Record*, Vol. 68 (New York: 1937) 12.

76   Berthold Ferrow, *Records of New Amsterdam 1653-74* (Baltimore: Gen. Pub. Co., 1976) 385.

77   *Melyn Papers, 1640-1699* (The Cornell University Library Digital Collection, 1993) 116-8.

78   Diana Gale Matthiesen, "Miscellanea regarding purchase of Staten Island," *The Melyn Papers, 1640-1699* (New York: New York Historical Society, 1914) 123-6.

79   Berthold Ferrow, *Records of New Amsterdam 1653-74* (Baltimore: Gen. Pub. Co., 1976) 169.

80   Ibid, 178.

81   Ibid, 182.

82   Ibid, 198.

83   Ibid, 225-6.

84   Ibid, 268.

85   Berthold Ferrow, *Records of New Amsterdam 1653-74* (Baltimore: Gen. Pub. Co., 1976) 198.

86   *Melyn Papers, 1640-1699* (The Cornell University Library Digital Collection, 1993) 127-30.

87   Ibid, 130-31.

88   Diana Gale Matthiesen, "Cornelis Melyn attends meeting, 23 May 1661," *The Melyn Papers, 1640-1699* (New York: New York Historical Society, 1914) 127-30.

89   Diana Gale Matthiesen, "Letter from Cornelis Melyn to West India Co., ca. 1661," *The Melyn Papers, 1640-1699* (New York: New York Historical Society, 1914) 119-23.

90   Diana Gale Matthiesen, "West India Co. letter re: Cornelis Melyn, 27 Jan 1662," *The Melyn Papers, 1640-1699* (New York: New York Historical Society, 1914).

91   Berthold Ferrow, *Records of New Amsterdam 1653-74* (Baltimore: Gen. Pub. Co., 1976) 48.

92   Ibid, 49.

93   Ibid, 50.

94   Diana Gale Matthiesen, "Miscellania regarding purchase of Staten Island," *The Melyn Papers, 1640-1699* (New York: New York Historical Society, 1914) 126-7.

95   Frank Baker, *Baker Ancestry: The Ancestry of Samuel Baker, of Pleasant Valley, Steubben County, New York, with Some of His Descendants* (self-published, 1914) 37.

96   Paul Gibson Burton. "Cornelius Melyn, Patroon of Staten Island and Some of His Descendants," *The New York Genealogical and Biographical Record* 132.

97   Ibid, 132.

98   *New Haven Town Records*, Vol. 1, 292.

99   Ibid, 450-2.

100 Ibid, 11-2.

101 "The Melyn Papers, 1640-1699," *Collections of the New York Historical Society for the Year 1913*. 97-138.

102 Paul Gibson Burton, *Cornelius Melyn, Patroon of Staten Island and Some of His Descendants*, Vol. 68. 138.

103 Clifford K. Shipton, *Biographical Sketches of those who attended Harvard College in the classes 1690-1700*. 298.

104 Ibid, 299.

105 Ibid, 299.

106 *Court Minutes of New Amsterdam*. 392.

107 Ibid, 339-40.

108 Ibid, 385.

109 Ibid, 409.

110 Ibid, 337.

111 Ibid, 337.

Bibliography

"Adriaen Pieterszen Van Alcmaer." *The New York Genealogical and Biographical Record.* Vol 7. New York: 1876.

Baker, Frank. *Baker Ancestry: The Ancestry of Samuel Baker, of Pleasant Valley, Steuben County, New York, with Some of His Descendants.* Chicago: self-published, 1914.

Bayer, Henry G. *The Belgiums: First Settlers in New York and in the Middle States.* Heritage Books, Inc.: 1987.

Broad Advice To The United Netherland Provinces . . . Made and Arranged, From Divers True and Trusty Memoirs, New-York Historical Society. The Cornell University Library Digital Collections, 1993.

Burt, Betty. *The Life and Times of Cornelis Melyn 1600-1674 Patroon of Staten Island New Netherland.* Self-published.

Burton, Paul Gibson. "The Antwerp Ancestry of Cornelis Melyn." *New York Genealogical and Biographical Record.* Vol. 67. 1936.

Burton, Paul Gibson. "The Antwerp Ancestry of Cornelis Melyn." *New York Genealogical and Biographical Record.* Vol. 68. 1937.

"Cornelis Melyn, Patroon of Staten Island and Some of His Descendants." *New York Genealogical & Biographical Record.* Vol. 68. New York: 1937.

Court Minutes of New Amsterdam.

Ferrow, Berthold. *Records of New Amsterdam 1653-74.* Baltimore: Gen. Pub. Co., 1976.

Fiske, John. *The Dutch and Quaker Colonies in America.* Boston and New York: Houghton Mifflin: 1902.

Inns, J. H. *New Amsterdam and Its People.* New York: Charles Scribner's Sons, 1902.

Kupp, Dr. Jan et. al, *The Early Cornelis Melyn and the Illegal Fur Trade.*

"Lord and Manors of NY." *The New York Genealogical & Biographical Record.* New York: 1908.

Matthiesen, Diana Gale. "Deed for Staten Island, 1640 [Cornelis Melyn]."
    The Melyn Papers, 1640-1699. New York: New York Historical Society,
    1914.

—. *http://dgmweb.net/genealogy/45/Melyn/MelynHome.htm.*

—. "Agreement between Cornelis Melyln and Lord Nederhorst." *The Melyn
    Papers, 1640-1699.* New York: New York Historical Society, 1914.

—. *http://dgmweb.net/genealogy/45/Melyn/Bios/JochemKuyterCornelisMelynin-
    NN.htm*

—. "The Cuyter-Melyn Mandamus of 28 Apr 1648." *The Melyn Papers,
    1640-1699.* New York: New York Historical Society, 1914.

—. "Power of Attorney by Janneken Melyen, 6 Apr 1656." *The Melyn Papers,
    1640-1699.* New York: New York Historical Society, 1914.

—. "Miscellanea regarding purchase of Staten Island." *The Melyn Papers,
    1640-1699.* New York: New York Historical Society, 1914.

—. "Cornelis Melyn attends meeting, 23 May 1661." *The Melyn Papers,
    1640-1699.* New York: New York Historical Society, 1914.

—. "Letter from Cornelis Melyn to West India Co., ca. 1661." *The Melyn
    Papers, 1640-1699.* New York: New York Historical Society, 1914.

—. "West India Co. letter re: Cornelis Melyn, 27 Jan 1662." *The Melyn Papers,
    1640-1699.* New York: New York Historical Society, 1914.

Melyn Papers, 1640-1699. The Cornell University Library Digital Collection,
    1993.

New Haven Town Records, Vol. 1.

Shorto, Russell. *The Island at the Center of the World.* New York: Vintage
    Books, April 2005.

Steinmeyer, Henry G. *Staten Island 1524-1898.* New York: The Staten Island
    Historical Society, 1950.

Made in the USA
Lexington, KY
12 April 2012